SpringerBriefs in Law

AF806337

More information about this series at http://www.springer.com/series/10164

Lutz-Christian Wolff

The Art of Law Teaching

Springer

Lutz-Christian Wolff
Faculty of Law
The Chinese University of Hong Kong
Shatin, New Territories, Hong Kong

ISSN 2192-855X ISSN 2192-8568 (electronic)
SpringerBriefs in Law
ISBN 978-981-15-9147-1 ISBN 978-981-15-9148-8 (eBook)
https://doi.org/10.1007/978-981-15-9148-8

© The Author(s), under exclusive license to Springer Nature Singapore Pte Ltd. 2021
This work is subject to copyright. All rights are solely and exclusively licensed by the Publisher, whether the whole or part of the material is concerned, specifically the rights of translation, reprinting, reuse of illustrations, recitation, broadcasting, reproduction on microfilms or in any other physical way, and transmission or information storage and retrieval, electronic adaptation, computer software, or by similar or dissimilar methodology now known or hereafter developed.
The use of general descriptive names, registered names, trademarks, service marks, etc. in this publication does not imply, even in the absence of a specific statement, that such names are exempt from the relevant protective laws and regulations and therefore free for general use.
The publisher, the authors and the editors are safe to assume that the advice and information in this book are believed to be true and accurate at the date of publication. Neither the publisher nor the authors or the editors give a warranty, expressed or implied, with respect to the material contained herein or for any errors or omissions that may have been made. The publisher remains neutral with regard to jurisdictional claims in published maps and institutional affiliations.

This Springer imprint is published by the registered company Springer Nature Singapore Pte Ltd.
The registered company address is: 152 Beach Road, #21-01/04 Gateway East, Singapore 189721, Singapore

I think teaching law is rather like herding sheep. You run around behind the students and bark at their heels, and head off the ones that start for the hilltops, and after a while, if you create enough commotion, they move down the valley and arrive at a destination without ever knowing how they got there. Of course ... whether it's the right destination is another question, and there is always somebody who wants to argue about that.

William L. Prosser, Lighthouse No Good, 1 Journal of Legal Education (1948), pp. 257–267 (264–265)

Preface

I have been a law teacher and I have practiced law in different jurisdictions for almost three decades. I have written this book because my law teaching experience may be worth sharing with others. I wanted to tell my stories hoping to be able to transfer some knowledge and skills, but also to provoke some discussion. My experiences, lessons and conclusions may not fit everywhere. But hopefully some of my thoughts can lead to reflection on how law is and should be taught and ultimately to improvements for the benefit of law teaching around the globe.

I am not aware of any publication which addresses comprehensively all those aspects which law teachers must consider daily inside and outside the classroom. This book aims to fill the gap by discussing law teaching from a great variety of angles.

I have written this book as a law teacher, i.e. not from an institutional perspective or the perspective of the representatives of any provider of legal education. Views presented in this book are consequently strictly personal and do not represent views and positions of my colleagues, Faculty or University. Furthermore, many of my observations are of course not law teacher specific but could be related to teaching in any subject area. This, however, is probably true for much that has been published on legal education topics and does not devalue the contribution to the field.

I have chosen a semi-academic approach for this book, i.e. rather than using research-based findings as the starting point I have tried to write this book in a personalized way. The focus is on my own teaching experience accumulated over the years. I have supplemented references to related legal education literature where available and appropriate.

Every law teacher has stories to tell. Many stories! We have funny stories, sad stories, embarrassing stories, juicy stories, disappointing and frustrating stories and sometimes stories which are too sensitive to report. For this book I have looked back and tried to record the milestone stories of my own law teaching history. I am sharing my stories because I think they are useful in the context of the discussion of specific law teaching themes, but also the bigger picture of legal education. Many of my stories relate to individuals for which reason anonymization and changes of story features were necessary. However, at the core all my stories are real.

I wish to emphasize that I cannot think of a more fulfilling and more satisfying way of earning a living than teaching law. I hope that this passion of mine comes across in the classroom and that it also comes across in this book. I am extremely grateful to all my students for always having been a great source of inspiration. Thank you! This book is dedicated to all of you.

Shatin, Hong Kong
October 2020

Lutz-Christian Wolff

Contents

Chapter 1
About This Book

This book aims to discuss different aspects of law teaching based on my own experience. I start by explaining why for me law teaching is to a large part an art rather than a science. This is followed by reflections on the goals of law teaching. The next chapters elaborate on the relationships between law teaching and research, skills training, and practical legal work. I am then trying to explore what good law teaching means or may mean.

The core part of this books concerns the question how law teachers prepare for class and how they should act and interact in the classroom. This concerns amongst other things the selection of course contents, teaching modes, teaching materials and teaching venues. When discussing the in-class experience I am trying to share many of my own tools and approaches. Some of them may appear trivial, but they have helped me and my students a great deal. Assessment is an important topic for students and teachers and a subsequent section therefore discusses related issues from the viewpoint of different stakeholders.

In most common law jurisdictions teaching evaluations are regarded as an important device to encourage self-reflection and to implement quality control. One brief chapter of this book is therefore dedicated to this topic. This is followed by thoughts on different aspects of the design of law courses, programmes and law school curricula.

The professional life of a law teacher is determined by her relationship with students, with other law teachers and with administrators. Three shorter sections consequently highlight key aspects of these important themes from different angles. This book concludes with remarks about the future of legal education in times of increasingly competitive legal markets, globalization and—most importantly—the use of legal technologies.

I have last verified online references in October 2020. I have omitted footnote citations in word-for-word quotes to improve readability. Some of the sections of this book are based on earlier publications or presentations as highlighted in the footnotes. Finally, I have tried to adopt gender-neutral language. However, it was not always possible to use the plural to avoid "she/he", "hers/his" and "her/him".

© The Author(s), under exclusive license to Springer Nature Singapore Pte Ltd. 2021

L.-C. Wolff, *The Art of Law Teaching*, SpringerBriefs in Law,
https://doi.org/10.1007/978-981-15-9148-8_1

For a change from traditional formats, I have therefore adopted the female format throughout except where quoting and when relating to real male persons.

My thanks go to Anja Chia for excellent proof-reading and to the publisher's team for being extremely supportive throughout.

Chapter 2
Law Teaching as an Art or a Science?

I once gave a presentation at a legal education conference organized by my own Faculty. During the Q&A session one of my colleagues asked me if in my opinion law teaching was an art or a science. I must admit that I was not really able to answer the question on the spot. I tried to rescue the situation by talking about the goals of law teaching and how law teachers can of course be regarded as artists of some kind. My colleague accepted my explanations with a knowing smile. He understood that I had never considered whether law teaching was an art or as a science. Like most of us I was just teaching my classes without much reflection on the theoretical or conceptual underpinnings. The title of this book seems to indicate that I have in the meantime made up my mind. However, things are not straight forward at all.

For whatever it is worth, a quick Google search shows that the differences between arts and sciences are discussed controversially around the globe. Often "art" is described as being concerned with beauty and good taste[1] and thus seen as the subjective expression of knowledge.[2] Art is subjective because it reflects different personalities, strategies, processes and preferences.[3] Also, art does not need proof. In fact, art-related knowledge cannot be proven and is therefore not about truth.[4] In contrast, science is seen as objective, evidence-based, theoretical[5] and concerned with

> general truths about the operation of general laws pertaining to the physical (and quantum) world and relies on methods of study and data accumulation based on observation and experimentation.[6]

Legal education research may not yet have reached the level of other educational sectors. In other words, for the time being legal education research remains a

[1] Cf. Hardison, https://www.enotes.com/homework-help/deference-between-art-science-172919.

[2] Ibid.

[3] Cf. Young, https://www.scotthyoung.com/blog/2016/04/19/art-v-science/.

[4] Koshal, https://www.differencebetween.com/difference-between-science-and-vs-art/.

[5] Ibid.

[6] Hardison, https://www.enotes.com/homework-help/deference-between-art-science-172919.

© The Author(s), under exclusive license to Springer Nature Singapore Pte Ltd. 2021
L.-C. Wolff, *The Art of Law Teaching*, SpringerBriefs in Law,
https://doi.org/10.1007/978-981-15-9148-8_2

niche area, although of course a very important one. And, this niche area is gaining momentum. An increasing number of studies attempts to address different aspects of legal education from a scientific point of view. My own research projects on various aspects of legal education have been real eye-openers and I can only encourage everybody to venture into some study about one's own teaching last but not least as a matter of self-reflection. All efforts of this kind are aiming at the same goal, i.e. to find out how law teaching can be improved and how perfect law teaching looks like. Research in legal education has in fact generated very valuable results. However, it remains questionable whether there is the one and only perfect way to teach law. In particular, it must be asked if law teaching is not also about beauty and aesthetics. Is law teaching driven by personal preferences of teachers and students, by different personalities? Is law teaching not often about strategies, processes and teaching tools which are adopted for rather irrational reasons, but very often with good results?

I was once invited to give a talk to practicing IP lawyers who were involved in law teaching in one way or another.[7] The topic I was supposed to address was how students can be convinced not to play with their iPhones or other devices during class, but rather to pay attention to the teacher. My conclusion was simple: if you are a good law teacher you will attract students' attention and they will abandon their electronic devices. This of course led to the much more fundamental question what the characteristics of a good law teacher are and what you can do to acquire those characteristics.[8] My answer was again straight forward: "There are people who are born teachers …and there are others." While this got me a big laugh, I believe until today that my answer carries a lot of truth. In fact, others have made similar comments.[9]

There are lots of aspects of law teaching which can be objectively assessed, and which can be learned. This probably is the scientific side of legal education. This book refers to many of these aspects. However, this book's focus is on the flip side of legal education. It is about teacher and student personalities, about enthusiasm and passion for and the beauty and aesthetics of standing in the classroom teaching law. In other words, this book is about the art of law teaching. One may of course claim that many of the related aspects can be and in fact have at least partly been explored and explained through research. While this is certainly true, I personally believe that good law teaching still involves a lot of subjectivity. And it is for this reason that for me law teaching is something arty. As a consequence, my personal stories, observations and conclusions which I set out in this book are admittedly very subjective. They can and they certainly will be challenged. I hope that this will make this book even more valuable.

---

[7] Wolff 2014.

[8] Also see *infra*, 7.3–7.8.

[9] Whaley, p. 1416.

Chapter 3
The Goals of Law Teaching

3.1 General

Any reflection on law teaching needs to start with a discussion of goals.[1] Why do we teach law and why do we teach law in a particular way? This question concerns at least three different aspects:

First, we must ask if teaching is really necessary. In other words, should we not rather leave it to students themselves to decide how they wish to achieve law learning outcomes through self-guided studies? Second, what motivates law teachers to teach, what motivates educational institutions to offer law programmes, what motivates governments to approve and support law schools? And third, what are the specific goals of law teaching in terms of learning outcomes? What do we want law students to take home from our teaching?

The first question about the value of independent learning will be addressed in a later chapter of this book.[2] This chapter addresses the second and the third question with a focus on the perspective of law teachers. In line with the spirit of this book the main considerations are based on my own experience.

3.2 What Motivates Law Teaching?

Motivation has been defined as "(i)nternal and external factors that stimulate desire and energy in people to be continually interested and committed to a job, role or subject, or to make an effort to attain a goal…"[3] From law teachers' perspective,

[1]Cf. also Peden, pp. 379–396.

[2]*Infra*, 7.8.

[3]WebFinance Inc., BusinessDictionary, http://www.businessdictionary.com/definition/motivation.html.

© The Author(s), under exclusive license to Springer Nature Singapore Pte Ltd. 2021

L.-C. Wolff, *The Art of Law Teaching*, SpringerBriefs in Law,
https://doi.org/10.1007/978-981-15-9148-8_3

what are the internal and external factors that stimulate the desire and energy to teach law?[4]

In interviews with early career applicants for teaching positions one can often get the impression that the only goal to start a teaching career is to save the world, i.e. to help students to become excellent lawyers with the ultimate goal to serve the society. In fact, I trust that many of us would love to regard ourselves as selfless, student- and society-focused, hard and diligent workers who are sacrificing their lives for the betterment of everything. But we also know that this picture is probably slightly out of touch with reality. In my whole career as a law teacher I have never encountered a law teacher who was a saint. I am afraid that the reasons for teaching law—like the reasons of other employees to go to work every day—are much more modest. Think about teaching relief. Teaching relief is available in many law schools e.g. for taking up a particular administrative role or as reward for success in teaching and research. The simple question is why teaching relief is so popular if everybody was just driven by the desire to make students fantastic lawyers? Should teaching relief not rather be seen as a punishment than a reward? Or did we rather get it completely wrong?

Although it may sound drastic, but realistically speaking law teaching is in the first place just a job like any other which allows us, the law teachers, to make a living. Fair enough one may say, but why would potentially highly qualified law school graduates decide to become law teachers while at the same time much more money can be made as practicing lawyers? Why do we teach law if we can get rich and famous as solicitors, as barristers, in-house counsels or even as judges?

Once upon a time, I met a lady in a bar in Hong Kong's notorious nightlife district Lan Kwai Fong. As the evening developed, she asked me what I did for a living. And, when I responded that I was teaching law, there was this sudden very disappointed feature in her eyes and she asked with disbelief: "But, don't only those who are not able to find jobs with law firms end up as law teachers?"[5] I do not have to explain that the conversation ended shortly afterwards. However, I am afraid the question of that lady carries at least some truth. Law teachers on the one hand and practicing lawyers on the other are often different breeds. We have different personalities which may have caused us to pursue different career paths. We have different career goals which determine why we are doing what we are doing.[6] Our personalities are of course also shaped by the kind of work we are engaged with. In other words, there are indeed reasons why some people teach rather than getting rich. There is of course nothing wrong with this, although it may lead to certain disadvantages when talking to strangers in Lan Kwai Fong. Furthermore, all this does not mean that we would not be able to practice law, although teaching does indeed require different skills, approaches and mindsets. Vice versa, I have seen practitioners who wanted to exit legal practice, took up a teaching job and have failed miserably. It is therefore quite clear that not all law teachers teach because they are unable to find jobs in the real

[4]Prosser, p. 259.

[5]Also cf. ibid., p. 259.

[6]Cf. ibid., p. 260.

world. We rather teach law because teaching law suits us better than practicing law and that this is for the benefit of our students. At least I hope so.

From the viewpoint of motivation there may be another difference between law teaching and practical legal work. Law teachers may prefer teaching over practicing law because there is less job security in private practice and because private practice may be more demanding in terms of time, workload, and stress. That said, it is a dangerous misperception that the job as a law teacher gives you lots of easy peasy lemon squeezy time and that there is no stress. Various sections of this book address the stress factor of law teaching and related aspects.[7] At this point it is sufficient to say that I have never encountered any law teacher who has been able to do just nine-to-five and not to work on weekends at least occasionally.

Some years ago, I read a fascinating novel about one of those great German writers who emigrated to the United States during the horrible Nazi regime in Germany. There was a particularly memorable conversation in that novel between the main character and another writer about the question why writers write. The answer the main character gave was that writers write because they want to be admired and loved by their readers. I trust the same can to a certain extent be said about law teachers. I have to admit that I feel extremely happy when a teaching session goes well and when students seem to like what I am doing, when I can see their sparkling eyes and when I can feel their questions and their attention. Vice versa, every law teacher knows the depressing sentiment when a session goes wrong. We have all had this experience. You get this terrible sensation of being disconnected. You realize that students look bored even though—if one is lucky—they may remain politely quiet. This kind of experience is terribly frustrating and has always pushed me to work even harder in preparation for the next teaching session. I did not want this to happen again, I wanted to be loved and admired by my students!

Do we therefore have to conclude that the motivation for teaching is at least to a certain extent vanity? Maybe! But if my vanity leads to an enjoyable in-class time and—as a side-product—to great learning outcomes on the part of my students, then I am happy to live with it. Actually, if this was really the case, we should all consider ways to increase our vanity levels to move our teaching to even greater heights.

Legal academics may of course not only be passionate about their teaching. Hopefully, they are also passionate about their research. So, this may also be a reason why they teach and why they teach well. They may want to promote their area of research and—not to be underestimated—get inspired by their students. Again, if this leads to good learning outcomes: great, go for it! In fact, I find law as a subject fascinating and I enjoy the interaction with my eager and critical students. This sounds very subjective. But yes, I must admit that ultimately my teaching is therefore driven not only by vanity, but also by selfishness.

Up to now I have only talked about law teacher motivation. The reason is simple: this book is by a law teacher for law teachers. Of course, one must consider other stakeholders as well. Most importantly, every law school[8] and every university have

[7] Cf. in particular *infra*, 9.2 and 10.2.

[8] Cf. Tan, pp. 67–79. .

their own institutional goals. These goals may not be completely aligned with the personal goals of individual teaching staff, but they are probably not less important. In modern times education has become an industry and often institutional goals will be or—in times of shrinking government support—have to be profit-oriented. Furthermore, the legal profession and the government have an interest in law teaching that maintains the quality of legal services. Finally, students do of course have a stake in the goals of law teaching. The motivations of different stakeholders may not be the same. However, in the end everybody aims to offer the best possible legal education, i.e. legal education that leads to the best learning outcomes. This is where the interests, motivations and goals of all stakeholders meet.

3.3 Learning Outcomes

The actual and desired learning outcomes of legal education in general and of programmes and courses have in the last decade been discussed widely. Many universities and law schools have adopted the so-called outcome-based education (OBE) approach.[9] The main questions nowadays are, if and how the outcomes of legal education can and should be defined and how these outcomes can they be achieved. How can it be ensured that law teachers teach in pursuit of pre-determined outcomes? At least in the common law world almost every law school nowadays requires programmes and courses to stipulate their learning outcomes. Some teachers define their own learning outcomes per course or even per teaching session. In line with good teaching practices, often this is conveyed to students at the beginning of each course or teaching session. But does this change the way a course is taught? Do law teachers really consider prescribed learning outcomes when delivering their teaching sessions? I must admit that I have my doubts and as I am writing these sentences a comprehensive research project[10] is under way at my University to assess related aspects. At this point I only wish to offer the following brief observation, which is again personal and very subjective.

Law schools need to decide for themselves whether they wish to educate legal intellectuals or train lawyers. In the last two decades law programmes offered at university level have more and more shifted from the former to the latter. This may be a result of the need to prepare law students for an increasingly competitive job market. And yet, I trust that it must be the goal of law schools to provide an education which fosters critical and creative legal thinking rather than just instilling legal knowledge and skills which graduates can apply in a robot-like manner when entering legal practice.

[9]The Education University of Hong Kong, https://www.eduhk.hk/flanobl/view.php?secid=784.
[10]Cf. Chan Ying Jenny.

> Or are we preparing the next generation of lawyers to be more flexible, team-based, technologically-sophisticated, commercially astute, hybrid professionals, who are able to transcend legal and professional boundaries, and speak the language of the boardroom?[11]

I strongly believe that critical and creative legal thinkers will eventually be the better lawyers. The goals and outcomes of legal education must be defined accordingly.

[11] Susskind, p. 162.

Chapter 4
Law Teaching and Research

Many law faculties offer teaching-only or research-only positions. Most law teachers around the world are, however, doing both, i.e. they are pursuing an academic career track which requests them to teach and to engage in research. How important is teaching for research active law teachers? How important should it be?

From an institutional perspective the answer is clear: Teaching is crucial for the success of any law school and should consequently be taken seriously. It is a different question if and how this understanding can and will also be enforced. In research led institutions one can often hear that for academic career advancement research must be outstanding while teaching and administrative contributions must (only) be fine. According to this philosophy bad teaching or bad performance in administration can be substituted by excellent research. In contrast, under-performance in research cannot be made up for with outstanding performance in the domains of teaching and administration. If this was really the institutional approach, then it would only be understandable for law teachers to invest less efforts in teaching. Law teaching would become a second-rate domain in academia, a necessary evil. While this may be the grim reality in some law schools, I trust that there are number of good reasons for taking a different approach.

From the institutional viewpoint good teaching is crucial to avoid obvious reputational risks. Even if internally teaching and administration are not given the same weight as research, the public view may be completely different and be led by the perception of teaching performance. This is not the place to discuss the international ranking game or the need to attract good students in order to sustain the financial viability of a law school. However, it is obvious that a damaged reputation in the domain of teaching can have far-reaching consequences.

From the law teachers' perspective, additional reasons should lead to the acknowledgment that that it is not wise to let the teaching just run on the side. First, as already mentioned, research can be useful for teaching and vice versa. Very often there is ample opportunity to use ongoing or completed research for course designs. This offers the teacher the possibility to talk about something which is important to her and about which she is passionate. It allows the use of high-level contents for teaching

© The Author(s), under exclusive license to Springer Nature Singapore Pte Ltd. 2021

L.-C. Wolff, *The Art of Law Teaching*, SpringerBriefs in Law,
https://doi.org/10.1007/978-981-15-9148-8_4

purposes. The preparation for class alone gives the teacher the chance to reconsider and restructure the research project from a very different angle. It also provides the opportunity to receive feedback from students whose ability to spot shortfalls and to provide input cannot be underestimated.

When I was a student, one of our professors once proudly explained his latest criminal law research findings in class. When the professor was finished one of my classmates who was known for his brains raised his hand and when the professor asked him to speak, he just said one word: "Wrong!" The perplexed professor produced a forced smile before he responded with also just one word: "Why?" It took my classmate five sentences to tear the professor's theory apart, who was quick to assure everybody that these were great ideas for a student which he would have to consider. He never mentioned his theory again.

Notwithstanding this story, teaching can indeed be inspirational from the research point of view. During teaching activities, I have developed many research ideas and most of my textbooks are based on my teaching. This is not at all surprising. As teachers we are forced to think issues through and to structure them properly or else it would not be possible to present them in a convincing manner in class. This kind of preparation enables us to understand gaps, inconsistencies and other aspects which deserve to be explored further. Feedback from and the discussions with students give further input.

Finally, another very important reason why teaching should be taken seriously is job satisfaction. Research is a very slow business. It takes months if not years from the start of a research project to the publication of the findings. It takes even longer to receive feedback, if at all. Teaching is very different. Every week the law teachers stands in the classroom attempting to make the class work. Students' reactions show promptly and clearly whether a class is successful. Hopefully, this is more often the case than not because, let us face it, being successful in the classroom is a very nice and motivating feeling while a class that goes wrong can haunt you for quite some time.[1]

[1] *Supra*, 3.2.

Chapter 5
Law Teaching and Skills Training

5.1 General

Legal skills are the techniques and abilities through which substantive law is applied in practice. Examples are legal research techniques, skills relating to the drafting of legal documents, the structuring of deals as well as presentation, communication, negotiation[1] and advocacy[2] skills.[3] In principle, substantive law education and legal skills training are two different things. In the past, at university level the focus has been on the teaching of substantive and—to a lesser extent—procedural law,[4] rather than on legal skills training.[5] However, the discussion whether law schools should train law students also in legal skills and to what extent has a very long history in particular in the US and has gained momentum also in other parts of the world. The question whether university level legal education should include skills training can be seen as being connected to the goals of tertiary legal education, i.e. if it is the goal of law schools to create critical and innovative legal thinkers or if we are in the first place (only) training forthcoming legal practitioners. I have already shared my point of view above.[6] I believe that it is not the task of degree programmes delivered at university level to churn out law robots who are trained to produce legal outcomes in an automated way. Law schools should rather aim at educating legal intellectuals in the best sense of the word, not least because this approach will create better lawyers.

[1]Cf. Bobot, pp. 13–22.

[2]Cf. Majid, pp. 39–58.

[3]The term 'legal skills' is not used consistently, cf. e.g. for the understanding of legal skills as law study skills Finch/Fafinski, p. 1.

[4]Cf. Boele-Woelki, p. 32.

[5]Cf., however, Macfarlane, p. v.

[6]*Supra*, 3.3.

© The Author(s), under exclusive license to Springer Nature Singapore Pte Ltd. 2021

L.-C. Wolff, *The Art of Law Teaching*, SpringerBriefs in Law,
https://doi.org/10.1007/978-981-15-9148-8_5

> The challenge arises from the difference between an education that aims to inspire students to think and an education that prepares them for the exercise of a profession.[7]

All this does not mean that skills training should be banned from the law school curriculum. Ideally law schools are committed "*both* to thinking *and* to professional training."[8] This is not just because a grasp of legal skills is important also to understand the substance of the law including its theory and its practical relevance. Furthermore, I had to discover through my own teaching that skills trainings are a perfect tool to teach substantive law as further explained below.[9]

5.2 Important New Legal Skills

This is not the place to discuss which skills should be taught at undergraduate and postgraduate level and in which manner.[10] However, apart from the traditional research, writing, presentation, communication,[11] negotiation and advocacy skills there are two specific skill types which are becoming increasingly important, i.e. skills related to legal technologies and skills related to legal entrepreneurship.

Legal technologies have been developed and continue to be developed further at a breath-taking speed over the past decade. Legal technologies are increasingly used by law firms and other providers of legal services.[12] Law schools need to prepare their students so that they can cope with these new features of legal work. Law students must have a basic understanding of topics such as[13]:

(1) Data analytics, artificial intelligence, automation and distributed ledger technology;
(2) Writing protocols for legal document analysis and composition;
(3) Ethical aspects of legal technologies;
(4) Cyber security and privacy protection in the context of legal technologies;
(5) Smart contracts;
(6) e-discovery, e-due diligence and e-contract review;
(7) e-document assembly;
(8) Cryptocurrencies and the law;
(9) Client management systems; and
(10) The use of legal technologies in dispute settlement.

Law teachers who can teach these topics and related skills are in high demand. Most law teachers of my generation may not even understand what these topics

---

[7] Post, p. 1819.
[8] Ibid., p. 1823.
[9] *Infra*, 5.3.
[10] Cf. Biggs/Hunter, pp. 1-30; Jones, pp. 35–48.
[11] Cf. Heinrich, pp. 99–130.
[12] Cf. *infra*, Chap. 18.
[13] Many thanks to my colleague Professor David C. Donald for his expert comments on this topic.

are about and will often not have the required in-depth knowledge to teach them. However, technology plays an important part in the lives of younger colleagues and certainly for the upcoming generations of law students. The ever-increasing significance of legal technologies does not leave any choice for law schools. Legal technologies must be part of any law school curriculum. Having said that, substantive law aspects of the technological developments are of course equally important.

The second skills topic law schools should push is legal entrepreneurship. Most of our students will pursue their careers in private practice. Only about 50% of the work in private practice is pure legal work. The other 50% concern office administration, business development as well as client and project management. Furthermore, some of our graduates will set up their own law offices. Sometimes this is done even right after graduation. In addition to the underlying legal knowledge, entrepreneurial skills and an entrepreneurial mindset are required to succeed in these domains, and it must be the task of law schools to lay the groundwork through related courses or even programmes. Surprisingly little attention has been given to this topic up to now.

In my course on "The Law of Cross-border Business Transactions" (LIBT) I always use one in-class exercise that aims to create awareness of the entrepreneurial side of legal work. The question paper gives instructions like these:

> You are an associate with the international law firm McGonners, Yeung & Francis (MYF). In a move to expand its service portfolio MYF has identified corporate social responsibility (CSR) as one of the possible growth areas. The managing partner asks you to explore the significance of CSR in international business transactions, to prepare a MYF Business Development Plan CSR and to present your findings to the partners meeting in ten minutes.

Year after year it is surprising to see how students struggle to work on this task. Business development is just not on their radar as it is not on the radar of law schools. There are very good reasons to change this.

5.3 Skills Training for Substantive Law Learning

I had mentioned above that I believe that skills trainings are perfect tools for substantive law learning. This section elaborates on this idea further based on my own experience when teaching my LIBT course.[14]

The decision to introduce (some) skills training modules to the LIBT course was originally driven by the desire to contextualize related substantive law by exemplifying how international business law works in practice and to loosen up the different teaching sessions. I soon realized two things: first, students seemed to enjoy the skills training exercises tremendously. In fact, skills training modules proved to be effective tools to overcome problems such as reluctance of students to engage in class and gaps in terms of knowledge and practical experience, different English proficiency levels as well as the cultural diversity of the student body. With the introduction of skills training exercises voluntary participation and interaction amongst LIBT

[14]Cf. for the following Wolff/Chan, pp. 81–109; Turner/Bone/Ashton, pp. 1–16.

students was no longer an issue. Second, their active involvement in skills training exercises encouraged them to apply and thus actively engage with substantive law topics if the skills training modules were designed accordingly.

I consequently decided to use skills training modules systematically as core teaching tools of the LIBT classes to facilitate active and sustainable learning of substantive law contents. At the same time, I had to acknowledge that the LIBT courses were not aimed and designed to provide comprehensive skills training. In fact, because of the limited time and because of the large size of the LIBT classes this would hardly be possible. The acquisition of some legal skills therefore just had to be regarded as a welcome by-product of the LIBT courses.

The ultimate design of the LIBT skills training modules developed over time and was a result of a trial-and-error approach based on considerations and acknowledgements which are discussed in the following.

To keep students' attention and interest over a whole term of 13 teaching weeks, the LIBT skills training modules had to be designed with the training intensity to be escalated week by week to 'maintain the momentum'. For this purpose, I designed the training pattern of different modules from 'simple' to 'complex' and I did this in two ways. First, I increased the complexity of the task, e.g. from 'passive' to 'active' and to 'interactive'. Second, an escalation of the skills training intensity was also achieved by increasing the difficulty of the substantive law problem students had to solve.[15]

To demonstrate how I have used skills training exercises for substantive LIBT learning purposes, one LIBT skills training module is reproduced in the following. For this exercise I divided students into A groups and B groups of up to 5 members each receiving different question papers. The groups were asked to negotiate their finalized draft versions with one group from the other category and to come up with a final negotiated version. The negotiated draft versions were presented and discussed in class during a de-briefing session. The group work was not assessed.[16]

QUESTION PAPER GROUP A
Kowloon Tong Trading Co. Limited ("KTT") is a Hong Kong company. To enhance the sales of KTT-products in the Netherlands, KTT intends to enter into an agency agreement with Dutch Amstelveen Agents Ltd. ("DA"). KTT's managing director wants "to make sure that DA is devoting all its services to KTT and will stay away from competitors". He asks you "to draft a clause for the agency agreement which appoints DA as KTT's agent for the Netherlands in relation to all KTT-products and protects KTT's interests in the best possible way." You are to negotiate your draft clause on behalf of KTT with DA-representatives in 20 min.

(continued)

[15]Cf. Whaley, p. 1402.

[16]Cf. for a different approach Clarke/Blissenden, pp. 368–381.

(continued)

QUESTION PAPER GROUP B
Dutch Amstelveen Agents Ltd. ("DA") has contacted you in relation to the conclusion of a distributorship agreement which DA intends to conclude with Kowloon Tong Trading Co. Limited ("KTT"), a Hong Kong company. Under the distributorship agreement DA shall "become KTT's distributor for all KTT-products in Europe" and DA wants to make sure "that DA has exclusivity in this regard"
The DA-CFO has asked you and your team to prepare a draft-clause for the distributorship agreement according to which "KTT grants DA exclusive distributorship rights for Europe in relation to all KTT-products." You are to negotiate your draft clause with the KTT-representatives in 20 min.

The instructions differ in that A-groups work on the basis that the agent is to be appointed for the territory of the Netherlands, whereas B-groups are instructed to draft a distributorship clause that grants exclusive agency rights for all of "Europe" which consequently had to be defined. Students were to find out about the differing goals of their clients only during the negotiations thus simulating a real negotiation scenario. As for substantive contents students had to address (i) the concepts of agency, (ii) distributorship and (iii) exclusiveness. The differing instructions forced students to consider and apply the underlying legal concepts. After an in-class discussion of the negotiated outcomes I presented draft clauses to students for benchmarking purposes.

This module built upon other modules which aimed to train students to draft legal documents. It escalated the training intensity by requiring students to develop their draft versions as group work and—for the first time—to negotiate their final product with others. Apart from a 30-minute introduction to basics of cross-cultural negotiations in an earlier session, students had not received any special negotiation training. I provided additional follow-up explanations on negotiation styles and techniques during the de-briefing session.

Based on in-class observations, surveys as well as informal discussions with students I was able to conclude that the main reason for the success of the LIBT skills training modules is rather trivial. Students simply enjoy the in-class interaction and were thus willing to take on a more active role and—if skills training modules were designed accordingly—to engage with the concerned substantive law concepts. Most of the LIBT students had never conducted any real (or simulated) practical work in international business law. The skills training exercises met students' eagerness to explore something new. Students also seemed to value the fact that I had designed the skills training exercises as real or simulated case scenarios, which offered training towards their ultimate goal, i.e. to work in private practice. The escalation of the skills training intensity maintained the inspirational momentum and reinforced the "sensation of moving forward" throughout the term.

I was able to observe that the excitement about the skills training exercises was shared even by those students who had initially taken a more reserved—not to say obstructive—approach perhaps because of their personalities, maturity, work experience or cultural background. Negotiation exercises seemed to be particularly helpful to overcome problems of this kind. It appeared that the competitive atmosphere took over and eliminated any pre-existing psychological and emotional barriers.

It is "... well established that students who are actively engaged in a learning activity will learn more than students who passively absorb information."[17] Observations in my LIBT class confirmed this conventional wisdom. The active work on substantive law issues as part of the skills training exercises led to a sustainable acquisition of knowledge which any passive mode of study could not have achieved. Furthermore, skills training exercises facilitated students' comprehension of any contextual features because the topic was explored in exactly such context. Finally, the student-to-student interaction in some of the skills training exercises reinforced "deep learning effects"[18] as students acted as teachers and learners at the same time.

Apart from drafting and negotiation training modules other LIBT skills training modules covered deal structuring, problem solving techniques and presentation skills.[19] I had also considered adding advocacy[20] trainings, but had to drop this idea due to time constraints. Nonetheless, skills trainings in advocacy as well as in presentation,[21] communication, interviewing,[22] conferencing and mediation skills could as well be very effective substantive law teaching tools.

As already indicated, variation seemed to be important. This did not exclude the possibility to repeat particular types of exercises, provided that the underlying fact pattern or the substantive law problem to be addressed differed. Negotiation exercises were especially popular among students, although it was at times difficult for the negotiation groups to generate the requested negotiation outcome. Often enough students had to be reminded that it was their task to produce results rather than being taken away by the fun of negotiating.

The introduction and use of the LIBT skills training modules had to overcome some challenges which I am addressing in other sections of this book and which I will therefore not discuss here. The greatest challenge was the class size of normally 60–80 students which made interactivity rather difficult.[23] Furthermore, the teaching venue, i.e. a big lecture theatre, was not ideal for group work.[24] But it did not jeopardize the use of skills training modules for substantive law learning altogether.

Finally, it is certainly easier to use skills training modules in a course on the "Law of Cross-border Business Transactions" than e.g. in a course on "Jurisprudence". However, for the reasons why they have worked in my LIBT course, I trust that skills training modules will work in other courses as well—even if more creativity is required for the preparation.

---

[17] Skead/Elphick/McGaughey/Wesson/Offer/Montalto, p. 366.

[18] Cf. *infra*, 7.8.

[19] Cf. Webb/Maughan/Keppel-Palmer/Boon, pp. 121–147.

[20] E.g. Pope/Hill.

[21] Cf. e.g. Boyle, pp. 189–238.

[22] Cf. Webb/Maughan/Keppel-Palmer/Boon, pp. 5–27.

[23] Cf. *infra*, 9.7.

[24] Cf. *ibid*.

Chapter 6
Law Teaching and Practical Legal Work

Many law teachers have never practiced law. Even though I believe that law must be regarded and should in the first place be taught as an academic subject,[1] eventually law teaching is meant to lay the grounds for students' practical work. In other words, law is a practical subject. Practical experience of law teachers therefore helps[2] and when consulted by students who wish to pursue an academic career, I consequently always advise that I regard it as beneficial to spend some years in private practice before returning to academia. I explain my reasons as follows.

First, a 24/7 job in a law firm toughens you up and thus increases your chances to survive in the increasingly competitive academic environment. Second, the professional interaction with clients, partners and other colleagues will of course strengthen the incumbent law teacher's social skills. Third, because law is a professional subject, legal concepts and norms are much easier explained when a teacher can link her teaching to her own practical experience, i.e. to share war stories. Last but not least, practical experience may give the law teacher credibility.

When I was still much more involved in legal consultancy work, I always tried to let students participate in my projects. Of course, I did so based on anonymity and with the utmost attention to issues of confidentiality. Students just love to hear about any kind of real cases. But real case scenarios are extremely helpful not just because they capture students' attention. They also demonstrate the practical importance of rules, concepts, and skills in real life contexts. Most of the in-class exercises which I use are therefore in fact based on real cases. I always explain to my students the background and I try to add some special personal feature to support the deep learning effect[3] by making the case and thus the substantive law content more memorable.

What if a teacher does not have practical experience? Does this mean that the real case scenario approach is unavailable? Certainly not! Real cases are everywhere. They are in case reports, in the papers and on TV or in stories of family and friends.

[1] *Supra*, 3.3.

[2] Cf. Kales/Ripley Thayer.

[3] Cf. *infra*, 7.8.

© The Author(s), under exclusive license to Springer Nature Singapore Pte Ltd. 2021
L.-C. Wolff, *The Art of Law Teaching*, SpringerBriefs in Law,
https://doi.org/10.1007/978-981-15-9148-8_6

Can you fake practical experience? Can you claim that you have worked on a particular case when you were not even close? I am sure you can, but there are two caveats. First, from an ethical point of view, fake stories which are sold as real are problematic. I do not think that it is justifiable to use fictitious stories without disclosing this in class. I would not do it and I think nobody should. Second, if you decide to fake a story, you better make sure that you are a good actor. The worst that can happen to any teacher is to lose the trust of her students. Even the slightest doubt that the teacher is pretending will lead to credibility problems and all the resulting difficulties to draw students back on the teacher's side.

Chapter 7
What Makes a Good Law Teacher?

7.1 General

It is rather obvious that good law teaching depends on good law teachers.[1] This section therefore attempts to discuss the credentials of good law teachers. I am trying to address this very difficult issue only from the law teachers' perspective. Law teaching can of course be affected by numerous factors, many of which are explored in other sections of this book. For example, badly designed programmes or courses will affect the teaching quality. Furthermore, the topic, the peculiarities of the student body as well as time, location, and venue of the teaching[2] are very important. Again, this section focuses only on the teacher herself.

7.2 Measuring Success in Law Teaching

Any discussion about good (or bad) law teachers involves judgements. And this is where the problems start. How do you assess the quality of teaching? How do you assess the quality of a law teacher? Is it a quality indicator that a law teacher is liked by students? But students' affection for a teacher does not necessarily imply that learning outcomes are being achieved. Is it a quality indicator that a law teacher receives good teaching evaluations? Teaching evaluations are very important for formative purposes and probably the best tool to assess teaching quality that is currently available.[3] But teaching evaluations do not provide watertight evidence on how effective the teaching has been, how much the students have actually learned and if prescribed learning outcomes have ultimately been achieved. Think about a very tough law teacher who is hated by her students because she is so demanding and strict as opposed to a law

[1]Cf., however, *infra*, Chap. 18.

[2]*Infra*, 9.7.

[3]Cf. *infra*, Chap. 12.

© The Author(s), under exclusive license to Springer Nature Singapore Pte Ltd. 2021

L.-C. Wolff, *The Art of Law Teaching*, SpringerBriefs in Law,
https://doi.org/10.1007/978-981-15-9148-8_7

teacher who takes a soft approach, who is funny, entertaining, patient and forgiving and has all the other characteristics which make a nice person. Do we really know that the latter is automatically better for our students? Is being hated as a teacher something bad even if the students probably benefit from the polarization, e.g. from the fact that the teacher's distinguishing features support sustainable knowledge acquisition?

There is of course a huge body of educational literature discussing different approaches to teaching and their perceived success. As mentioned earlier,[4] it appears to be the goal of all the writings to find and promote the perfect way to teach, i.e. in our discipline the perfect way to teach law. Legal educational literature has indeed made valuable contributions. However, there are also good reasons for considering legal education research with a degree of caution.

In my personal and therefore again rather subjective experience, some colleagues who do research on legal education topics are excellent teachers, but others do simply not reach that level.

> There is an old and popular saying, which stems from Bernard Shaw, that those who can do, do, and those who cannot, teach—to which, in deference to our university departments of education, professors in general have added that those who cannot teach, teach teaching.[5]

You may argue that the theory of a philosopher does not have to be wrong just because the philosopher herself does not adhere to her own words. And yet, it leaves a strange feeling if somebody tries to tell you how to teach best but is unable to apply her own wisdom. There simply is a credibility issue.

The second point is that those of us who are conducting research in legal education and in other areas of law are admittedly not just driven by the sublime goal of finding perfect solutions. We rather want to be and—for career advancement purposes—must be successful in terms of research. To achieve this goal, we must ensure that our research findings are acknowledged. In other words, our research becomes our product, and our findings are our selling points. Unfortunately, this may sometimes lead to peculiar dynamics. We need to publish, we need to get citations and—the latest trend—we need to generate impact. The question is what this means for the ultimate goals of our research.

Consider the case that somebody has developed a new law teaching tool, conducted underpinning research for a considerable period and has even used this teaching tool in class. How likely is it that this somebody will conclude that the teaching tool does not work after having made all the investments in terms of time and energy? Which journal would publish an article reporting on this failed attempt? I am afraid that it must be accepted that if you nurture a baby you will hardly admit that it is ugly. Nothing more needs to be said about the unfortunate consequences of the pressure to generate impactful legal research.

Finally, and most importantly, very often when I attend talks about teaching pedagogy or when I read about related themes, I find all this very interesting. However, how do we know that it really works? As mentioned at the outset of this section, generating reliable evidence of the success of law teaching is a very complex undertaking.

[4] *Supra*, Chap. 2.

[5] Cf. Prosser, p. 259.

Maybe it is even a mission impossible. Let me explain this point with reference to the research that I have conducted with my co-investigator, Jenny Chan, in relation to the Flipped Classroom (FC) concept.[6]

In essence the FC concept means that the lecture is moved online, and all in-class time is used for interactive learning activities.[7] What was previously the homework will be done in class under the FC concept. What was previously done in class, i.e. the lecturing, will be available outside the classroom.

I had adopted the FC concept for my LIBT class[8] seven years ago. To assess if my FCs had worked, we had to determine what "worked" meant for me and my students. We decided that this was a matter of teaching success evidenced by improved learning outcomes. To measure these learning outcomes, we relied on three different methods.[9] First, we compared my teaching evaluations with earlier ones, i.e. with teaching evaluations of LIBT course deliveries which had not used the FC approach. While I was of course happy that the scores had remained equally high, this did not really help us to understand if there was anything good about using FCs. This is because my teaching evaluations simply did not say anything about what students had learned in my class. Second, we counted the number of visits of the online lectures by students. This allowed us to understand at least that almost all students had watched the online lectures and not simply ignored the instructions to prepare for class. In fact, many students had watched the online lectures several times. However, we also had to acknowledge that this information did again not help us in deciding if FCs led to improved learning outcomes. Finally, in each year at the end of the LIBT course we asked students to complete a survey in order to find out what their views on FCs were and what challenges they had experienced, if any. The responses we got were mostly positive, although part-time students complained about the additional time, which they had to spend on the course.[10] Unfortunately, again we had to conclude that this was all very nice but did not reveal if students had learned more or better as compared to times when I had not yet adopted the FC concept.

It appears that the only way to really understand if the FC concepts leads to better learning outcomes is to compare the knowledge and skills of students who have been taught on the basis of this method with those who have not. We have considered this option, but eventually had to decide against it for the following reasons.

First, we considered comparing exam results. But exams can of course not be the same in different years and it is almost impossible to assess if the level of difficulty is the exactly same for different exams. Second, the student body differs year on year, i.e. while admission requirements may remain unchanged, it is impossible to assume that the student quality is 100% identical in each year.[11] And then there is also the

[6] Cf. Wolff/Chan; for the FC concept *infra* 9.3.

[7] Wolff/Chan, pp. 9–13.

[8] Cf. *supra*, 5.3.

[9] Wolff/Chan, pp. 99–107.

[10] Also cf. Tarrant, pp. 64–80.

[11] Wolff/Chan, p. 98.

person who sets and marks the exams, i.e. the course teacher. My Faculty has given up bell-curve marking some years ago in order to comply with the outcome-based approach, and all of our teachers are trying their best to be objective. However, how can we exclude the possibility that we are still—at least subconsciously—marking according to what we think our classes deserve in terms of rough percentages per grade in each year? In other words, if in a particular year students' exam performance in my class is below my expectations, would I really give everybody lower grades or would I rather consider that my exam was too difficult or that my teaching had not prepared students properly for the exam? Again, I am not saying that this is what is happening. In fact, when marking exam papers, I keep reminding myself that I am to assess objective outcomes rather than students' relative performance. But strangely enough, the grade distribution in my courses is roughly the same year after year.

I normally teach my LIBT course twice to two cohorts, i.e. there is a morning class and also an evening class. For the FC research, Jenny Chan and I had considered to use the FC concept only for one of those cohorts so that we would be in a position to compare student performance in the same year on the basis of the same examination. However, we had to abandon this idea as well mainly for two reasons. First, there is an ethical issue. If the FC teaching is better or worse than the "normal" teaching, how could we justify that only half of the students would benefit or suffer from this new approach? Second, there would still be the question of comparability. The evening class is reserved for part-time students, whose situation is obviously rather different from the situation of full-time students. Furthermore, the evening class normally has different dynamics compared with the morning class.[12] This may be the result of the fact that the teacher and the students are tired from the day and are looking forward to the well-deserved glass of wine after class. In fact, my own teaching evaluations for the evening class are always slightly below those of the morning class.

To sum up, collecting hard evidence to show the success (or failure) of law teaching in terms of improved learning outcomes is challenging. In line with the theme of this book I will therefore in the following sections present my personal views without being able to rely on hard evidence.

7.3 Different Teaching and Learning Cultures

When talking about teaching law and studying law, generalizations are as common as they are dangerous. Teaching and learning cultures do not just differ significantly from country to country. They also differ within countries and even between law schools of the same city. As law teachers we must take this into account and be careful when considering what might and what might not work in particular contexts. This does not only concern the obvious such as the sensitivities in particular societies in relation to political themes, gender issues and the teacher-student relationship in

[12] Cf. ibid.

general.[13] More importantly, the cultural background of teachers and students may have a significant impact on their teaching modes and learning styles.

The precise meaning of "culture" is of course heavily disputed and discussed broadly everywhere. It appears that there is common understanding that at its core, culture means something like:

> … historically evolved values, attitudes and meanings that are learned and shared by the members of a given community, and which influence their material and non-material way of life. Members of the community learn these shared characteristics through different stages of the socialization process within institutions such as family, religion and society as a whole.[14]

Libraries offer bookshelves after bookshelves of publications discussing the cultural determination of human behavior in different circumstances and in particular in the context of teaching. This is not the place to discuss this further. However, it is important for law teachers to remember that different cultures may lead to and may require different approaches, i.e. approaches which differ also from their own. These different approaches may have their own merits in particular circumstances and may sometimes be more suitable, while other approaches may not be appropriate and thus not work for one reason or another.[15]

When I was teaching law in Germany, I had a very bright female student. She was always late, always came barefoot because—as she later explained—she "just wanted to try one summer barefoot", she always brought a huge dog and often a follower who herself was not even a law student. I liked this scenario as this student was so different from her classmates. And much to the annoyance of the rest of the class, this student was extremely intelligent.

As I try to make all my classes very interactive, I would normally call upon students to answer my questions, to make suggestions and to develop solutions even if the session is supposed to be delivered in the lecture mode.[16] When inviting this student to answer my in-class question, I would first look at her for a moment, then I would say in a rather flirtatious way—as I now realize—"Frau Suchandsuch!?" and she would reply with a not less flirtatious smile "Herr Wolff!?", after which we would discuss the legal issue. The student later graduated from a different university as number one in the whole state. She is now something like a celebrity in Germany because she also excelled in non-law related areas, and when I checked some years ago, she was even listed among the 300 most influential persons in Germany. I am still trying to convince myself that my teaching has contributed at least a bit to her success.

Why did I tell this story? I had to learn that my rather flirtatious way of interacting, which had worked very well in Germany, would not be viable in Asia.[17] In fact, also in Germany this may not be acceptable, but back then nobody cared. I must admit that

---

[13] Cf. *infra*, 9.8, 10.5 and 14.

[14] Tayeb, p. 10.

[15] Wolff 2018, pp. 21–24.

[16] Cf. for in-class interactivity *infra*, 9.4.

[17] Cf. also *infra*, 10.5.

in those times I simply lacked the awareness that a teacher should probably never be flirtatious in class nor after class, for that matter! Anyway, my point is that different approaches may only work at particular times and in particular environments. In fact, what works in one place may even get you into serious trouble in other places. It is mandatory to keep this in mind and to choose your teaching style accordingly.

7.4 The Law Teacher Qualification

Law teachers' qualification must be considered from three different angles. First, there may be formal requirements. Second, there is the soft skill qualification. And finally, there is also the question how qualified a teacher must be in terms of substantive knowledge.

Universities and law schools operate within different frameworks setting out the requirements for law teachers to teach.[18] Do you need a law qualification or could you teach at least certain law subjects if you (only) hold degrees in sociology, politics, economics or history? Do you need a PhD? In which circumstances do you allow external part-timers to teach? Do you allow PhD students to teach, and if so, are there any special requirements? What about governance and quality control? These are all very important questions which require careful consideration, but they are outside the scope of this book, which focuses on the perspective of law teachers.

There appears to be a general (mis-)perception that everybody with a qualification in law can teach law. Sometimes teaching even seems to be regarded as the easy way out for anybody who is tired of private practice. In fact, many extremely successful law teachers have joined academia from private practice. But, there have also been other cases, cases of practitioners who have not become successful teachers, maybe because they did not think their teaching engagements through, because they had not considered that law teaching is hard work which requires meticulous preparation, or because they had not imagined that students are sometimes even more demanding than clients.[19] In these cases, the main reason for failure was that law teaching was normally not regarded as serious business that requires knowledge and skills.

> Once in a while, and worst of all, the dean has foisted upon his law school a loafer, a lazybones who finds that a modest salary with six or eight hours of teaching a week and three months of vacation every summer is the life of his dreams, who goes fishing, who plays golf and grows roses, who takes a good long nap every day after lunch and two hours of lunch before his nap, and never does anything at all.[20]

[18]Cf. The University of Chicago Law School, Paths to Law Teaching, https://www.law.uchicago.edu/careerservices/pathstolawteachingte; Yale Law School Career Development Office, https://law.yale.edu/sites/default/files/area/department/cdo/document/cdo_law_teaching_public.pdf.

[19]Prosser, p. 260 ("almost as stupid as clients").

[20]Prosser, ibid., p. 259.

As mentioned before,[21] some people are natural teachers, others already have teaching experience in other areas, e.g. as football coach, creative writing instructor or just as parents who have worked with their kids. But there are also people who have no teaching experience and who have no talent to teach! Does this prevent them from becoming successful law teachers? I do not think so. Law teaching can be learned at least to a certain extent, and I am trying to share many of those things that can be learned in this book. But there are also deal breakers. It is difficult to imagine someone who cannot speak in front of a large audience to become a successful teacher. I am talking in another section of this book about the stress which many of us feel before and during class, and how this may hinder successful teaching or—in a best case scenario—how stress may indeed bring out the genius.[22] But, if somebody is not able to overcome the stress at all, then entering the law teaching profession is certainly the wrong career move.

> I wish that I could convey to anyone who never has sat in the perilous seat the trepidation, the dismay, the feeling of helpless inferiority, with which a new professor looks into all those fresh young faces ... which are regarding him with such manifest skepticism and disapproval. It is a solemn and awful thought that he alone is to be responsible for getting somehow into their heads the course which he has with such difficulty succeeded in getting into his own. I have heard of men who, in that situation, turned and fled and were never seen in a law school again.[23]

The other type of failed teacher is the over-confident one who has a completely wrong understanding of how she or he comes across and how she or he can communicate. This teacher type is unable to connect with students. The situation can be remedied, but it requires self-reflection and the difficulty lies in the fact that the problems are related to the teacher's personality.

How qualified do you need to be as a law teacher in terms of substantive knowledge. The senior partner of the law firm that had hired me for my first job once called me into his office to give me a lecture on how to do deal with a particular client enquiry in an area in which I had no expertise. "Herr Wolff," he said, "I am able to familiarize myself with any area of law over a weekend at least to the extent that I can talk to the client. Once I am working on the matter, I will write an article or even a book, because this will force me to structure my knowledge and enable me to sell my expertise to other potential clients appropriately." The amazing aspect of this story is that this partner was not lying. His track record showed that he had not made something up, although one may of course question if his is the correct lawyering approach. I also need to mention that this senior partner was and is a fascinating man with an impressive personality, not just because he was able to work himself into a legal topic in such a short period of time. He is in his seventies now, still practicing and still as charismatic as he has ever been. I have learned a lot from him.

What does this story mean for law teachers? I trust that all law teachers can teach subjects within their area of expertise. This is in particular true if there is enough time

[21] *Supra*, Chap. 2.

[22] *Infra*, 10.2.

[23] Prosser, p. 262.

to prepare. The unfortunate reality is, however, that it is sometimes also necessary for us to teach courses outside of our comfort zone due to institutional needs. This does not necessarily mean that the teaching will not be successful. In fact, I have seen colleagues who—based on their broad experience—only needed half a day to prepare for a teaching session in any field of law if they had access to related materials. In these circumstances their teaching may not have been the best of the best, but it was up to the required standard. Not everybody can do this. I can certainly not claim to be that efficient. However, I also believe that with sufficient preparation time it should be possible to deliver teaching in core areas at a standard which students can expect.

It is of course a completely different question whether it makes sense to allocate teaching to teachers who have no prior expertise in the related area. In this regard a fine balance must be struck between teaching allocation needs, teacher satisfaction and well-being, the need of early career academics to develop a teaching portfolio which is not confined to niche areas, the expectation that every law teacher should be able to teach core area courses and the need to address emergency situations. Obviously, in a perfect world every law teacher just teaches in her own area of specialization. In reality this perfect world does not exist. In particular in emergency situations, e.g. when a teacher suddenly becomes unavailable, but the course cannot be cancelled, it may be necessary for a teacher to get familiar with a new teaching subjects on very short notice.

When I started teaching in Hong Kong, I ended up teaching—as far as I remember—ten different courses in my first academic year. All topics were new to me. I had to prepare each course from scratch, i.e. I could not rely on pre-existing course materials. Two half courses had to be taught in Mandarin. I was working day and night for that year and often I was indeed not more than half a day ahead of my students. The teaching allocation to me in that year was probably not perfect, but I survived, and I learned a lot. The preparations for my courses allowed me to build up a teaching portfolio on which I can rely until today. Most importantly, I gained confidence in my own teaching abilities.

7.5 The Law Teacher Personality

Trying to assess if law teachers have any common characteristics and if there is even something like a law teacher personality, will lead to nowhere. Law teachers are human beings, and they are as different as people in any other profession. Again, colleagues may have a personality which makes it easier to succeed in class. These are the born teachers. And then there are the others. As mentioned before, I trust that many law teaching techniques and skills can be acquired, although this may take some time.

Law teaching is challenging because law teachers, like teachers in any other discipline, must play at least four different roles. Law teachers have to be knowledge acquisition facilitators and skills trainers, actors, entertainers as well as role models.

First, it is rather obvious that as teachers we have to instill knowledge and skills in our students. I believe that this does not mean that we should spoon-feed our students. But, this is a different story which I will address further below in another section.[24]

Second, law teachers must also be actors! In every single teaching session, our students expect us to perform at the highest level. They do not understand if we explain that we have slept badly last night and that it is therefore difficult to concentrate. They are in no position to appreciate that we are grumpy because we are trying to lose weight and have therefore not eaten for a whole day. They are not concerned with major career considerations which are bothering us or any other matters which may distract us and cause us not to deliver our teaching at the highest level. Have you ever tried to explain in class that today's teaching session is particularly difficult for you because of some personal reason? Or have you even apologized for your teaching not being as good as it should be? Don't try! Trust me, it will not work. Students may understand that teachers are human beings. But they still want their show and in fact they are entitled to get their show. If you have bought tickets for a concert and the singer forgets her text you may be understanding if you hear that she had a rough day because her flight was delayed and she has consequently not been able to rehearse properly. But you will still be disappointed and unhappy about the money you have wasted. It is the same with students. They have expectations and we need to do everything to meet these, provided that they are in line with the prescribed learning outcomes.

It is on the other hand obvious that we cannot always be in top form. This is simply impossible. And in these situations, we must act. We have to pretend that we are 100% concentrated and engaged, that we are full of passion for the topic even if we regard it as the most boring thing in the world and we need to laugh about our own jokes although we have told them again and again for the past ten years. We also have to join students when they are having fun doing in-class exercises, although we may really not be in the mood. We just need to put up our show day after day and week after week. This is our job and most of the time it works. Most of the time!

Third, I trust that it cannot be said that law teachers must be entertaining.[25] But it helps if they are. Law is perceived a very dry subject. I believe that this is not true, and it certainly does not mean that our classes have to be boring as well.

Many of the law lectures I attended as a student were indeed terribly unexciting. However, for a couple of years every Friday afternoon a judge was giving lectures on decisions of the German Federal Court of Justice. This judge was a fantastic teacher. He was extremely inspiring and serves as my own role model and personal hero to this day. No need to mention that he was extremely knowledgeable and able to explain difficult legal issues in a very simple and clear way. More importantly, he was ridiculously funny. Nothing like that had ever been seen before at my alma mater. Friday after Friday, this judge's lectures were packed with 500 plus students with all sorts of backgrounds, from beginners all the way to graduates who were back

[24]*Infra*, 7.8.

[25]Cf. Offer/Skead/Seen, pp. 135–153.

just for the fun of it. Within five minutes of the lecture the whole venue was filled with roaring laughter while seconds later everybody was highly attentive because the judge had moved on to serious legal business before he would crack the next joke. When I attended these lectures, I promised myself that if I were ever to teach law, I would want to be like that judge. While my students know better, I think I am doing okay in terms of being informative and entertaining. But I also must acknowledge that I have never been able to get even close to the level of that judge. He was just amazing.

Finally, as law teachers we are also role models for our students. "Students both learn how to think and acquire professional training by forging personal psychological connections with individual faculty."[26] Students will always observe how teachers perform, how they behave, how they present themselves.[27] If a student is pursuing an academic career it is likely that she will remember her favorite teachers and try to follow their footsteps. Just like I will try all my life to be as good as that judge I spoke about before. However, I am convinced that we are not only role models for the very few who wish to become academics. Every week when we stand in the classroom, students are checking us out, considering if there is anything they should adopt or avoid. As teachers we carry authority qua position.[28] After all we are running the show. Students are not only copying the way we deal with legal problems. They also consider how we speak, write and present ourselves, how we are dressed,[29] how we interact with others and how we address challenges. As teachers we also have a lot of power in terms of opinion building. Students are willing to give serious consideration to what we say on law and other topics as well. This is the nice thing about being a law teacher. We can (still) shape our students. Of course, this is also a huge burden, and we need to remind ourselves not to be too imposing.

7.6 Toughie Versus Softie

Teachers are not equally strict. Being tough on students or taking a soft approach may reflect the teacher's personality. But this certainly does not have to be the case because teachers can as well pretend to be toughies although they are not and vice versa.

Early career law teachers sometimes think that being softer earns them their students' affection and—probably more importantly—gets them better teaching evaluations. In fact, a harmonious relationship with students sounds like something every law teacher wants to achieve. But, being liked or not liked is only one side of the story. The other side concerns the question if the toughie or the softie is the better teacher. Does a tough teacher achieve better learning outcomes than a teacher who

---

[26]Post, p. 1823.

[27]Cf. Whaley, p. 1395.

[28]Cf., however, Liu, pp. 146–164.

[29]Cf. *infra*, 9.8.

always tries to please students? Is a teacher who is hated by students because she is too demanding automatically a bad teacher?

An unreasonably tough teacher has no place in the law classroom. If the requirements e.g. in terms of preparations for class, in-class participation and exam performance are unreasonably high, then the responsible teachers are abusing the trust laid in them by all stakeholders including and most importantly by their students. Vice versa, a teacher who is not demanding at all may as well look for something else to do. Law teachers must set goals for students and ensure that these goals are being reached. And this conclusion also answers the question whether tough or soft law teachers are better: it does not really matter as long as the learning outcomes are achieved. I have talked about different teaching and learning cultures in the previous section. Law teachers and the providers of legal education have indeed very different styles. Student groups are very different. The approach to be taken may therefore differ significantly and sometimes it must differ if required by the circumstances. Furthermore, variety is of course a valuable commodity in legal education. From a pedagogical point of view, students who are exposed to different teaching and learning environments will learn how to cope with these differences and thus be better prepared for the real professional life which also offers diverse settings. This also means that every single teacher must find the right approach for herself, for each topic taught, for each student group in each setting.

But how about student perception? Is it true that students like the softie and hate the toughie?

Some years ago, during one of our orientation sessions for our new students I was introduced by one of my colleagues as "a killer". Yes, correct! As "a killer"! This immediately got me a lot of attention from the students present and forced me to declare for the records that the grades my students receive are completely in line with the average grades awarded in other classes. My teaching approach, which my colleague described as "killer-approach", is of course outlined in many sections of this book. But some additional remarks are necessary in the context of this section.

I am tall, relatively fit and completely bald. I think I look tough and I know it. This has advantages for example in class as students normally accept my authority without any questioning. It is more challenging in other situations, e.g. when I come to the negotiation table and the other side immediately takes the defense position because I look so uncompromising. All this can easily be overcome with a smile, which comes naturally in-class when I am doing what I enjoy most. I must admit that it is more difficult when I sit in boring meetings, but this is again another story.

And yet, I am strict in the classroom. I believe in interactive teaching and I have learned that it does not make much sense to wait for students to raise their hands to answer my questions. This simply takes too much time for a number of reasons. Students may feel shy, they may not be sure if they know the correct answer or they may not want to be seen as trying to please the teacher. Moreover, it is normally always the same group of students who volunteers to answer the teacher's questions while we want to ensure that everybody is participating. So, I walk through my class and call upon different students and I do this irrespective of the class size.[30] I explain my approach to my students during the first teaching session and I continue to communicate with students about my teaching style throughout the whole course. I even explain again and again that I understand that it may often be more convenient for students to be left alone. At the same time, I also state that it is easier for the teacher to just lecture. But, from the "deep learning" perspective,[31] which I explain in class, interaction is what is needed. And it is more fun. I rarely had a problem with this approach.

I remember the first proper law course I ever taught was "Private Law for Non-Law Students". The class time was Monday mornings from 8:15am to 10am. About 500 students showed up for the first class and they were all still there for the last session 12 weeks later. Despite the large number of students, I adopted the same teaching style, i.e. I still called upon individual students to answer my questions. And it worked! I knew that my approach put students under enormous stress, because speaking up in front of 499 classmates is not easy. However, I made it clear that there are no wrong answers and I made sure that everybody who was called upon would eventually get a "Very good! Well done!" I learned later that the son of the friend of one of my neighbors had also attended this course. He told his father that after every single of my lectures his shirt was completely wet because he was sweating so much for fear that I would ask him one of my famous questions. But he confirmed that my course was excellent and that he just loved it.

Much later, I had already moved to Hong Kong, a new colleague was about to join our faculty from private practice. I invited him to sit in my class to get a feel of what teaching in my Faculty was about. After class he told me that he was shocked how hard I was on my students. But, I explained my approach and he agreed that students seemed to know me, that they did not appear to be bothered and that each of the interactions with any of them ended with "well done, very good" or some other encouraging remark.

I think I am demanding, but I also try to be understanding. I firmly believe that students appreciate if and that they are treated like adults and not like children. This approach works for me and it works for my students or else my teaching evaluations would not be what they are. Students may regard me as tough because of my teaching style. But my style works for me and my students in terms of learning outcomes, so I believe. At the same time, I acknowledge that completely different approaches may work for other law teachers and other student groups.

There is another point which I think is important. As teachers we are leading the class. As explained in the next section,[32] I am very much in favor of independent learning and I believe that we should pass much more responsibility for their success in law learning to our students. But, in the end it is the law teacher who determines how to conduct a course. Students must understand this. I am sometimes very clear about this in class when dealing with students who try to be a bit uncooperative. I

[30] Also cf. similar Whaley, p. 1390.

[31] Cf. *infra*, 7.8.

[32] Ibid.

bluntly ask them: "In this class ultimately who is the boss?" My question normally eases any tensions, everybody has a good laugh and we can carry on. But it is indeed important not to forget that the teacher should never give up leadership. It is for the law teacher to guide students' learning.[33] What this exactly means can of course differ tremendously depending on the situation.

> Sometimes leadership requires adamant inflexibility … and sometimes it requires endless agility. Sometimes an effective teacher must be cautious and appreciative of the wisdom of existing arrangements, and sometimes a leader must be audacious and willing to crack eggs. Sometimes leadership requires cunning, sometimes confidence. Context is everything.[34]

I have still not answered the question if the softie law teachers get better teaching evaluations. I do not have empirical evidence at hand, but I had reported earlier about my reputation as a tough teacher. In one student blog, a student who had spotted my photo somewhere asked who I was. The answer from another student was prompt: "He is a law professor, very demanding, but very good!" There you go. In fact, my teaching evaluations have always been excellent. I have won the Vice-Chancellor's Teaching Excellence Award of my University three times and also the University Education Award. And all this despite my reputation as a killer.

One last remark: the softie vs toughie theme is of course also important in the context of assessments. I will discuss assessments in a later chapter,[35] but wish to mention here that reasonably difficult exams have their advantages. They are fairer, because difficult exams allow the better students to show how good they are, and they allow the marker of the exam paper to easily distinguish between good students and even better ones. Again, it makes sense to explain this to students while at the same time ensuring that it is understood that any exam will be fair.

7.7 Non-arty Characteristics[36]

I had explained at the outset that I believe that law teaching can be regarded as an art because of the subjectivity involved.[37] There are, however, also other characteristics of law teachers which may determine the quality of their teaching and are beyond personal choices. I am talking about age, looks (incl. height, body weight, baldness, hair, and skin color etc.), ethnicity, gender, accent. Many studies have attempted to demonstrate to what extent these and other features are determining how a person is perceived, and there is no reason to believe that this should not also apply to law teachers. I do not have empirical data, but I have explained in the previous section that my own appearance (tall, relatively fit, completely bald, senior white male)

---

[33] Also cf. *infra*, 10.16.

[34] Post, p. 1817.

[35] *Infra*, Chap. 11.

[36] Many thanks go to Prof. Samuli Seppanen for informative discussions on this topic.

[37] *Supra*, Chap. 2.

seems to give me some natural authority in the classroom.[38] But I can imagine that e.g. early career law teachers, who may hardly be much older than their students, can find it difficult to establish a similar presence in the classroom at first. Do other unchangeable characteristics such as gender and race of the law teacher have the same effects? Could be, and this is certainly worth further research. According to my own experience and observations, however, ultimately a teacher convinces through her knowledge and the way how she gets this knowledge across to her students. Despite any personal features of the law teacher, students will soon make their own assessment as to whether the teaching is worth their time or not. This does not exclude the possibility that certain personal characteristics of a law teacher are advantageous or disadvantageous. It only means that these characteristics can be overcome, towards the positive or the negative.

Two aspects require some further discussion:

First, conventional wisdom and convincing anecdotal evidence has it that experience as a law teacher in general and in relation to a particular course are important factors which positively affect law teaching. This is not surprising. Somebody who teaches a course for the first time will be less familiar with the topic, will know nothing about potential problems and questions students might have and will not yet be in a position to determine which delivery mode is most suitable. I often advise younger colleagues who are upset about their first teaching evaluations[39] that the situation normally improves significantly when a course is taught a second or even third time. I also remark in this context that the "normally" is important and that improvement is always the result of dedication. I have in fact seen cases where teaching evaluations worsened over time if a course was taught for too often e.g. because the teacher becomes over-confident or loses the enthusiasm for the course.

Second, many law teachers teach law in a language other than their mother tongue. Does this affect their performance? Does a posh Eton accent or a broad Texas drawl give the teacher an advantage at least over non-native speaker law teachers? My feeling is that this may indeed be the case, depending on where and to whom you teach. But, since only few language super-talents can easily switch from one accent to another, we probably must live with this acknowledgment.

When I flew to the US for the first time, I made the mistake of ordering a black coffee on the plane. I had to repeat my order three times until the very patient flight attendant finally understood. I must admit that this experience got me very worried about my English, only to discover after touch-down in New York that many people there spoke with an even heavier accent than I did. In fact, being a native English speaker does not guarantee that you are understood.

I have taught in German, which is my mother tongue, in Mandarin and I am nowadays normally teaching in English. I think my first teaching in Mandarin was a complete disaster.[40] Upon reflection, language may not have been the only issue,

---

[38] *Supra*, 7.6.

[39] *Infra*, Chap. 12.

[40] *Supra*, 10.1.

there was also the complete lack of experience. It is the way how you build short, but punchy sentences, how you repeat your messages, how you insert breaks and—most importantly—how you engage the audience.

As a matter of principle, teaching with an accent does therefore not matter. In fact, students will benefit from being exposed to different accents, as the globalized legal work environment will demand exactly that. If the language is clear, the presentation is well-structured, and contents are properly covered, nobody will have an issue with a foreign accent. ... almost nobody. I often get the feeling that my German students in Hong Kong do not like my Germany accent. When considering potential reasons, I must admit that it may be something cultural. When studying in a foreign country, I would probably want to get what I think is the real McCoy as well. And that may not be a German accent. But there you go. My students just must bear with me.

7.8 Helicopter Teaching Versus Independent Learning Approaches

Modern legal education is student-centered or at least it pretends to be. "At all stages of the process, the *students* should be the teacher's central concern. ... You, the teacher, face the important task of servicing their needs. It is not about you. It's about them."[41] The question is what this really means. Do all our teaching efforts have to focus on students? How about focusing on the law teacher for a change?[42] And, while it must be acknowledged that some of law students are underage, most of them are adults who can get married, can have kids, can in many countries become soldiers and go to war and vote. Who are we to think that we must and can provide around-the-clock care to our students? Furthermore, is student centeredness not counter-productive in the sense that we are hindering our students to grow up and become mature lawyers? Finding answers to these questions is not easy. I will try to explain my position in the following, based on three stories and related observations.[43] The first story relates to an email received by one of my colleagues some years ago. The email went something like this—no kidding:

"*Dear professor,*

I am a new student and I really need your help. I know that I must get an A in your course but have no idea how to achieve this. I am working very hard and I am willing to do anything to secure a good job after graduation. But, I am not sure what to do. And, since competition is tough and as I also have three other courses this term I do not want to make a wrong move. I know that I do not have any time to waste. Therefore, can you please answer the following questions:

[41]Cf. Whaley, pp. 1388, 1397.

[42]Cf. *infra*, 7.9.

[43]I had first presented these stories at the CUHK Teaching and Learning Expo in December 2013.

(1) *For the examination, do I have to read all the recommended readings or is it enough to learn your power points? If I only learn the power points will this be sufficient to get me an A, an A- or which other lower grade?*
(2) *Is there any book from which I can study which guarantees that I will get an A in your course?*
(3) *Is there anything that I can do to get a better grade than other students of your course?*
(4) *What exactly do I need to do to write an essay which receives an A grade?*
(5) *Can I send you sample essays so that you can have a look at them and tell me how I can improve to get an A?*

Thank you in advance for all your answers. I apologize for any inconvenience, but my parents expect me to excel and I do not want to disappoint them.

Best regards,

Your student"

For copyright and privacy reasons I have changed the email, but in substance it is what the colleague had received. I will leave this story uncommented for now and move on to the second story.

The second story is my own story. It relates to my experience as a student. When I started law school, we were taught in classes of up to 1000 students. Students were sitting on the stairs of the lecture halls and often the lectures had to be videoed so that students could follow the screened version in another venue. Moreover, in my days, professors would hardly ever hand out lecture materials. Lectures were normally not at all interactive. The professors would just talk. In fact, I felt that most of my professors were not good at teaching. They were so bad that for the last two years prior to the final state examination I did not attend any lectures as this was time-consuming and did not really help much. I had rather drawn up my own study plan and worked in the library or in small self-study groups for those two years, supplemented by up to three mock exams per week. In those old days there was also not much contact between students and the professors. Until I attended the oral part of the first legal state examination, I had only spoken twice to one of my law professors in relation to a scholarship matter. Otherwise I would not have dared to approach them, but I also did not see any need to do so.

When I started teaching in Hong Kong, I was quite surprised—not to say shocked—at what was required here: small class teaching, preparations of piles and piles of lecture notes, regular meetings with academic mentees and so on. And I asked myself: "Are Hong Kong universities really teaching adults? What is the difference between university teaching and kindergarten care in Hong Kong?"

And this leads me to story No. 3. which was reported in a local Hong Kong newspaper some time ago. It goes as follows:

It was discovered that many Hong Kong kids from richer families apparently assume that watermelons are red. Why? Because at home there is a domestic helper. And the domestic help prepares the watermelons for the kids' consumption. As a result, all these kids only see the red edible inner part of the watermelon and it does of course not occur to them that in reality watermelons look different.

These are just three little stories, but I could add many more. My stories lead to one very important question: Should we not teach our law students how they themselves can discover that watermelons are green?

To answer this question, we need to remind ourselves what the goals of law teaching at university level are. I trust that everybody agrees with my earlier statement[44] that the goal of law teaching is not just knowledge transfer. We do not aim to produce law machines that are able to perform automated legal services. We rather want our teaching to produce critical, innovative, and creative thinkers across disciplines. And to achieve this goal we wish to encourage the famous "deep learning".

"Deep learning" has been a very sexy term for decades. If you used this word, you were immediately recognized as a member of the inner circle of those who understand what education really is about. Normally the deep learning approach was understood as one which fosters active engagement with the subject matter and encourages students to

- aim to understand material for themselves,
- critically engage with substantive knowledge,
- link ideas to previous knowledge and experience,
- discover and use organizing principles to integrate ideas,
- establish links between evidence and conclusions, and
- assess the logic of arguments.[45]

Deep learning is contrasted with surface learning which leads to not more than the reproduction of information.[46]

Note that in recent years the meaning of deep learning has changed. Deep learning is now understood as a sub-discipline of machine learning "concerned with algorithms inspired by the structure and function of the brain called artificial neural networks."[47] This book is of course not concerned with machine learning[48] and the traditional understanding of deep learning is therefore adopted throughout.

Deep learning is certainly not encouraged by spoon-feeing students. Deep law learning is not a result of helicopter teaching in law schools. Quite the opposite, helicopter teaching creates immature students who rely on the helping hand of their university teachers as they have relied on their parents and on all that hand-holding at kindergarten level and in primary and secondary schools.

If it is our goal to encourage deep learning, then we must strive to create independent learners. In fact, in a perfect world independent learners are learners who do

---

[44]*Supra*, 3.3 and 5.1.

[45]Lublin, https://ctl.byu.edu/tip/teaching-deep-learning. The idea of deep learning was apparently first shaped by Marton/Säljö, pp. 4–11.

[46]Lublin, ibid.

[47]Brownlee, https://machinelearningmastery.com/what-is-deep-learning/.

[48]Cf., however, Chap. 18.

not need teaching. They organize themselves, they arrange their learning activities independently, which would be an important part of their reflective self-education process. In a perfect world we as law teachers would therefore stop our teaching efforts. At best, we would set and administer exams, probably a few lectures or tutorials which show students how to organize their studies and how to learn. But even this could be done by students themselves and it would help them tremendously! Law schools should be very happy about this kind of approach, as the operation would become very cheap. No classrooms would be required, and no teachers would be needed. And in the end all law teachers would lose their jobs.

Of course, all this sounds a bit drastic. I am not promoting the end of law teaching. Law teaching in Germany in my student days may again serve as one example why such an approach may neither be desirable nor work. As mentioned, in my student days we were just thrown into the sea of law studies and it was either swim or sink. There were and to this day there still are many law students who sink and drown. Up to 25–30% of those who take the First Legal State Examination to graduate from law school do normally not pass.[49] Many others do not even get that far and quit earlier. I have seen many German law students ending up in emotional trouble. All my law school friends agree that the preparation for the First Legal State Examination was one of the toughest and cruelest challenges in our lives. To this day I sometimes wake up at night because I have dreamed about the oral examination when one of the professors was banging his fist on the table, yelling at us that it was unbelievable that really nobody in the examination room knew the answer to his question.

I still believe that my law studies were a good experience. They taught me that I can teach myself to swim. Everywhere!

Maybe my observations at the outset should encourage us to take a critical look at our own teaching approach. The question we need to ask ourselves is whether we are doing enough to educate our students to become independent learners? How can we improve? Which measures can we adopt to foster independent learning? What this means precisely may differ tremendously depending on the circumstances. It may differ from course to course, from teacher to teacher and from student body to student body. But there are also many points which are valid across the board.

Law teachers should not teach answers, but questions. And law teachers should help with the independent development of the answers. The Socratic teaching method[50] adopted in many law schools in the US students does exactly that. It promotes guided self-studies with in-class time used for students to apply their knowledge by answering questions about the relevant topic. There is no lecturer who (just) lectures. The FC concept adopts a similar approach.[51]

To sum up, helicopter teaching is certainly not in the best interest of law students nor of students of any other discipline. Spoon-feeding does not have any advantages

---

[49]For 2017 and 2018 the failure rates were 28.72 and 27.94%, cf. Legal Tribune Online, https://www.lto.de/jura/studium-zahlen/erste-juristische-staatspruefung/.

[50]Cf. Kerr, pp. 113, 134; Schneider, pp. 26–29; Garner, pp. 1597–1649.

[51]Cf. *supra*, 7.8, and *infra*, 9.3.

and does not even improve the teacher's teaching evaluations. Unfortunately, spoon-feeding is what many think is or should be expected from law teachers. Things will not change overnight. Not even after this book is published. But this should not stop us from asking ourselves how we can empower our students to be independent learners. Whatever the answer to this question is, it must be understood that the starting point is always law teachers' and students' mindset. Law teachers must not be seen as knowledge transferors, but rather as learning facilitators!

7.9 Motivating Law Teachers?

With all the modern student centeredness law teachers receive much less attention. In fact, law teacher motivation is not really discussed at all. But if law teachers are not motivated, then law schools really have a problem. And law students do as well. Why then is law teacher motivation apparently completely ignored?

One may argue that law teacher motivation is not important, because students are adults and they should consequently be able to learn independently, as discussed in the previous section.[52] One may further consider that de-motivated law teachers may even be a good thing, because de-motivated teachers are potentially bad teachers and this forces students to engage in independent learning. But, while independent law learning deserves of course to be encouraged, the notion of de-motivated law teachers may not be in line with the teaching and learning culture in most modern law schools.

Law teacher motivation is important to ensure good teaching. Motivation is, however, not a guarantee for good teaching. Even a highly motivated law teacher can be a disaster in the classroom. Furthermore, the importance of teacher motivation for good law teaching may indeed be overrated. You can be a very good teacher without being motivated. Yes, you can! You can, provided that you are able to "act" like a motivated teacher based on your experience or based on good training that you have received.[53]

Teacher motivation is important for teachers' well-being. De-motivated teachers are normally not happy teachers. Teacher motivation is also important for students' well-being. Again, this seems obvious, a grumpy teacher can be very frustrating for students. Finally, teacher motivation is also important for the well-being of the institution, as it contributes to the building of a positive institutional culture.

All these reasons why law teacher motivation should be given proper attention may sound trivial, but they are not. They require acknowledgement and action, but are often overlooked in the busy reality of law teaching.

Motivation is of course first an issue for law teachers themselves, i.e. it is about teacher self-motivation. Self-motivation also implies steps to avoid de-motivation.

[52] *Supra*, 7.8.

[53] *Supra*, 7.5.

And nothing is more de-motivating than a class that goes wrong! It is therefore extremely important to consider all the issues which I am trying to flag in this book.

When talking about teacher motivation one may also have to consider what role students have to play in this context. It is rather obvious that low-performing, disinterested or even misbehaving students will in most cases have de-motivating effects on the teacher. But can we go even one step further and say that students also have a responsibility to motivate their teachers? In fact, if students go to university to study law, to learn from their teachers, then they can probably be expected to do everything to achieve their goals. Motivating their teachers—not just the other way round—could be part of this. Again, this idea is certainly not in line with the modern notion of student centeredness and even if it was accepted, it would require a lot of communication and student-teacher relationship training as well as probably even a major change of the direction of legal education. But take for example the online teaching which is currently conducted around the world to address the risks caused by COVID-19. Despite gentle invitations and even strong reminders, most students do not turn on the video function. As a result, teachers are talking to black boxes, which is—as everybody will agree—a sub-optimal experience at best. Is there not a role for students in supporting their teachers?

From an institutional perspective, objectives, strategies, and tools to motivate law teachers fall within the broad spectrum of good management practices and organizational behavior, which have been researched as far as the corporate world is concerned for very long. In contrast, it unfortunately seems that this issue has hardly received much attention as far as higher education is concerned although there are important and interesting questions to be addressed. Just a simple example: In the corporate world you can fire unmotivated employees. This is much more difficult at universities. Prosser has pointedly commented on the comfortable situation of a law professor in this context as follows:

> … short of flagrant immorality or similar misconduct—in which I am happy to say that few professors of law have ever been caught—he is immune from removal or discharge. No other business or profession could operate under such rules, and no other has need to.[54]

I trust that everybody agrees that in the end student motivation is more important than teacher motivation. However, the fixation on student centeredness as it has developed over the past decade(s), should not prevent any discussion of how the teaching environment can also be improved for law teachers. Motivated law teachers make a difference not just for themselves, but also for students, for their employers and for many other stakeholders.

[54] Prosser, p. 259; also cf. Post, p. 1818.

Chapter 8
Law Teaching and Fitness

Law teaching can be extremely tiring, and fitness is therefore an issue. Three aspects must be considered in this context, i.e. mental fitness, physical fitness and—as a special aspect of physical fitness—the teacher's voice. Fitness is of course important for any kind of job and I will therefore keep my comments short. Furthermore, the following brief remarks are of course not about how to set up a fitness plan for law teachers or to discuss what kind of sports is best, although it is obvious that basketball would come out on top. This section is rather meant to reinforce the idea that we need to be prepared for class in many ways.

First, physical fitness. Every law teacher knows how tiring just a one-hour lecture can be. If you teach for three hours or—as I normally do—two three hour sessions on the same day, then you sometimes struggle to stay concentrated during your sessions and afterwards you are really ready for a beer. I remember when I started this teaching pattern in Hong Kong with the second teaching session ending at 9:15 pm, I was so exhausted that I was unable to get anything done for the whole next morning. Also, I have checked this, I lose up to two thirds of a pound in each three-hour teaching session. I also remember times when I got dizzy and had to sit down during class because I was just too tired. Teaching is physically challenging, and fitness helps!

Moreover, I argue that physical fitness affects the way how a law teacher teaches and how good the teaching is. Is the teacher you just standing behind the lectern or even sitting in front of the class and could it be beneficial to take a different approach? I found that in-classroom active teachers, i.e. teachers who move around in the classroom and use lots of body language, are the more effective teachers, not least because students regard them as energetic and engaging. In contrast, the (traditional) lecturer who talks down to students from behind the lectern is out. I am sure this can be proven through one of those impressive empirical studies—if this has not been done already—which assess the impact of teacher movement in the classroom on learning outcomes. For me, it is just experience. Experience as teacher and as former student. Having said that, I acknowledge that generalization never works in all circumstances. One of my former colleagues would always enter the classroom, take a deep breath, and then lecture for the whole in-class session

© The Author(s), under exclusive license to Springer Nature Singapore Pte Ltd. 2021
L.-C. Wolff, *The Art of Law Teaching*, SpringerBriefs in Law,
https://doi.org/10.1007/978-981-15-9148-8_8

non-stop. As far as I remember, he hardly moved, but remained behind the lectern in front of the class all the time. Interestingly, he always received very high teaching evaluations, because his explanations were extremely well-structured, sharp, and very, very interesting. He just was a brilliant lecturer. This does of course not mean that he could not have been even better had he shown more physical presence in different corners of the classroom.

A special feature of physical fitness is the teacher's voice. In the past for some time I always lost my voice in autumn, i.e. right at the start of our academic year. I only recovered after two to three months. I am not sure what the reasons were. Doctors were not able to help, although of course they carried out all sorts of expensive tests. You feel completely helpless when you are without voice. And when you must teach in such a situation, you wonder whether you have chosen the right job. I survived, but each lecture is a real torture.[1]

I never use microphones when I teach. I do not like the big ones because I use a lot of gesturing when talking with my students and therefore need my hands free. I also do not like the small ones, the ones that you clip to your suit or to your tie and which come with a cable that leads to the cigarette box-like thing which you have to put into one of your pockets. I can accept that the sharp edges of the clip may damage my suits or ties, and that the cigarette box thing will do terrible things to the pockets of my expensive suits. But when I heard about that professor who forgot to turn the mini mic off when he went to the bathroom during the lecture break, I decided that this business was far too risky.

My university offers voice training courses delivered by an opera singer to post-graduate students. This sounds like great fun and could be very useful. In fact, there are many possibilities how you can train your voice. I have never done anything like this but admit that perhaps I should have. Nobody is perfect!

In addition to physical fitness, law teaching does of course also require mental fitness. From this perspective, lecturing is easier than any kind of interactive teaching mode which require you to respond to students' action or inaction.[2] When lecturing you can just carry on talking without even considering the presence of an audience. It normally takes rather long until students express their dissatisfaction, e.g. because you are too fast, too slow, too boring or because you just fail to make your point. In other words, you can completely focus on your presentation and ignore the students in front of you. You can, but even when you are lecturing you should of course not do so.

Do law teachers have to be fitter than teachers in other subject areas? Yes, of course! Law is not only the most interesting subject one can think of, but also the most challenging one. Teaching law is therefore most demanding physically and mentally. And yes, this point just had to be made once and for all. … although just tounge-in-cheek for now.

---

[1]Cf. Oseid, p. 176.

[2]*Ibid.*, p. 181.

Chapter 9
Preparing for Class

9.1 General

Unless a law teacher is a genius, proper preparation for class is the key to successful teaching. Even for classes which I have been delivering for over 15 years, I still need between one to five hours to prepare for every teaching session each week, depending how difficult it is to check for updates and which new developments have taken place since I taught the class last time.

I have spoken about my experience when I first started teaching in Hong Kong and had to prepare and teach many new courses from scratch.[1] I learned in those very tough times that—if push comes to shove—I can prepare a three hour class from scratch in one day net. This is very hard and requires a lot of concentration, but it can be done. Again, I can only speak for myself and I know that generalization is dangerous. Other colleagues are faster or slower. And of course, the preparation time depends on the topic, how much background knowledge is available, the level at which the course is taught and the teaching mode. Ultimately, it is the goal of any preparatory efforts to ensure that the teacher is able to deliver the course as it is supposed to be delivered. This includes that the teacher has superior knowledge of the subject taught and is familiar with the teaching mode. There is no real magic to it. You need to know your stuff and you need to know it well. Moreover, you must have a workable concept how you will deliver your teaching session.

Proper preparation for classes is hard work! While outsiders often do not (or do not want to) understand this, law teachers know this all too well. However, we also know how rewarding a successful teaching session can be (for students and teachers!) and that just for this reason it is worth to invest time and energy.

---

[1] *Supra*, 7.4.

© The Author(s), under exclusive license to Springer Nature Singapore Pte Ltd. 2021

L.-C. Wolff, *The Art of Law Teaching*, SpringerBriefs in Law,
https://doi.org/10.1007/978-981-15-9148-8_9

9.2 Selecting Topics

There are normally limits to the possibility of law teachers to select the topics they wish to teach.[2] The curriculum[3] requires core subjects and elective courses to be taught, there are normally only so many teachers with expertise in particular areas and different colleagues have different preferences as to which classes they which to deliver. The selection of the courses to be offered in a particular year and the corresponding allocation of courses to particular teachers is normally done by an academic colleague, e.g. the Programme Director, the Associate Dean (T&L) or by the Dean. In practice, very often also administrators play an important role, because teaching allocation is to a large extent a matter of administrative feasibility and logistics. When I was tasked to do the teaching allocation some years ago, another colleague dryly remarked: "You will be the best hated man in the Faculty!" It was not all that bad, but it came close. Teaching allocation is such a special experience because it is virtually impossible to make everybody completely happy, in particular because core teaching needs must be met. Patient communication, equal treatment of everybody and transparency are key to ensure cooperation and support. But even this does not always work. When I was in charge of teaching allocation, I remember one rather extreme encounter caused by the allocation of a course to one teacher in his area of expertise, but at postgraduate level which he did not like. I refused to make the requested change, as this would have required changes also to the teaching allocation of other colleagues. My refusal provoked a rather strong-worded reply. I invited the colleague to write to the Dean (not me in those days), the Dean simply asked somebody else to take over that course and I looked pretty stupid.

Apart from personal preferences, law teachers may have to pay attention to the courses they teach also from a career perspective. First, building up a rather broad portfolio of courses improves employability at the current and other institutions. Somebody who for her whole life has only taught niche subjects may find it difficult to find employment elsewhere unless a need in exactly those niche areas arises. I always advise younger colleagues to obtain teaching expertise in at least one of the core areas, e.g. in contract, torts, company law, criminal law, constitutional and administrative law. Actually, I recommend that younger colleagues should strive to teach equity and trusts, because law teachers who enjoy teaching this subject are rare and therefore teaching needs often exist in this area. I must admit I have not been too successful with my recommendation so far.

I have touched upon the relationship between research and teaching in an earlier section.[4] Teaching in the teacher's own research area is of course easier because of the expertise and because of the (hopefully) also existing passion for the subject. But I also know many colleagues who have never ever taught in their main field of research. And this is not only for those who research exotic topics. I am not saying that this is good or bad, but it happens.

---

[2]Prosser, p. 262.

[3]Cf. Friedland/Hess.

[4]*Supra*, Chap. 4.

The selection of a course to be taught by a particular teacher is also important for teaching evaluations. Difficult subjects may lead to bad teaching evaluations, whereas perceived fun elective courses which are only attended by a smaller number of students may generate better student feedback. It is difficult to say which subjects are difficult and which are not. For example, as mentioned above, normally equity and trusts is regarded as a torpedo course that is hated by students, who will consequently issue terrible teaching evaluations. However, in my faculty one of my colleagues has been able to prove this general assumption to be wrong. Nobody knows how he does it, but with his equity and trusts course he is one of the teaching superstars in terms of student feedback.

In my faculty we have observed another phenomenon. One would assume that undergraduate courses are easier to teach, because freshmen are inexperienced, innocent and generally nice. For us, however, it is the other way round. Even colleagues who have always received top teaching evaluations in postgraduate courses may be virtually smashed by the student feedback they get for their undergraduate teaching. We are not sure about the reasons, but it leads to the strange situation that colleagues might prefer teaching at postgraduate level even though they are more demanding.

Finally, a particular course may not run if the institution has set a certain viability threshold in terms of student numbers. This can lead to problems for the teacher who has been assigned to teach that course in a particular year. First, all the preparations may have been in vain at least for this year, and since she is not teaching at full load, potentially more teaching is owed to the faculty in the future. Whether challenges of this kind can be avoided or overcome depends on the situation on the ground and may differ significantly between institutions. But law teachers have to be and are aware of this issue.

9.3 Teaching Modes

9.3.1 General

Law can be taught in many ways, e.g. as lecture, in the lecture plus tutorial mode, supplemented by micro-modules, by flipping the classroom, through distance learning, in block courses and in the co-teaching mode. The teaching mode can be key to success (or failure) of a course. Different teaching modes may be more suitable depending on the circumstances such as the topic, the teacher personality, the student body, the venue and so on. Therefore, teaching preparations may also require considerations about the teaching mode. I am saying "may require" because sometimes the teacher does not have a choice. This can e.g. be the case when the teaching mode is prescribed by the institution or by the course leader. For example, in many law schools, undergraduate courses are taught in the lecture plus tutorial mode and this does not leave much room for the teacher to maneuver. Moreover, bigger classes are often taught in different sessions by different teachers, and a common teaching mode may be adopted to ensure a harmonized course delivery. Before getting to certain aspects which deserve some discussion in this regard, some more general features of teaching modes must be considered.

As mentioned, often there is no choice. But even if options regarding the teaching mode are available, the teacher may simply ignore those and do what law teachers have done for centuries, i.e. just lecture. Lecturing means that the law teacher explains, and students listen. Modern teaching pedagogy is rather critical of conventional lecturing because lecturing forces students into passivity. The argument is that lecturing does not foster deep learning.[5] Students are not encouraged to engage proactively with the taught themes.[6] This does certainly not mean that the lecture mode is dead.[7] First, it is of course also possible to lecture in an interactive way. Even when lecturing, I am in constant communication with my students and I understand that many colleagues are doing the same. I had also already mentioned one of my former colleagues who did not subscribe to any interactivity, but caught the attention of and inspired his students through his brilliance.[8] It is, however, important for law teachers to be aware of the available alternative options, i.e. that the lecture mode is not the one and only way to deliver a class and that other teaching modes might have their own advantages.

When law teachers consider teaching modes, they first need to make a general, but very conscious decision how much they wish their students to engage in independent learning. I have made my point before.[9] For many good reasons the more independent students learn the better. Spoon feeding is not the way forward!

As also explained before,[10] it is extremely difficult to assess the success of law teaching and the same is of course true for different teaching modes. Reports on the great success of particular teaching modes must be considered with care.

We were once honored with the visit of a professor from overseas who had announced a lecture on FCs.[11] He showed us technically perfect videos of in-class teaching sessions where students were asked about and actually discussed certain legal issues. Beautifully done, really! It was obvious that a lot of money had been spent on the production. Also, he kindly indicated that he would of course be very happy to allow us to buy his videos if we really thought that they might support our teaching. The session took an unfortunate turn when the professor was asked about his definition of FCs. He simply could not provide one. Instead, he kept reminding us how beautiful his videos were, although the pedagogical concept underpinning such beauty was not all that clear. As one of my colleagues remarked, Hollywood style video clips maybe very entertaining. But whether they can lead to improved

[5] Cf. *supra*, 7.8.

[6] Cf. ibid.

[7] Cf. Wolff/Chan, pp. 16–23.

[8] *Supra*, 8.

[9] *Supra*, 7.8.

[10] *Supra*, 7.2.

[11] For the FC concept cf. the following.

learning outcomes is a very different story. And of course, we did not purchase any of those videos.

9.3.2 Modern Teaching Modes

There has been a lot of discussion in recent years regarding the introduction of innovative teaching modes and tools. Funky terminology is used to describe different approaches, while clear definitions are often missing and the underlying concepts remain blurred or are overlapping. Some of the core concepts and terms are mentioned below. It must be remembered in this regard that most of the terms are not technical terms and that a harmonized or even unified usage does not exist. Furthermore, my list is of course not exhaustive. There are many other approaches which may have their own advantages.

- FCs: in-class time is traditionally used for lecturing whereas homework is for exercises. The FC concept "flips" this approach by moving the lectures online, i.e. outside the classroom, whereas in-class time is reserved for exercises. In other words, in-class time is for enquiry, application and assessment.[12]
- Inverted classrooms: this term is normally used as synonym for FCs.[13]
- Blended learning: means "the integration of face-to-face and online instruction".[14]
- Hybrid learning: is normally used interchangeably with "blended learning". Some educational writers insist, however, that "at first sight hybrid learning and blended learning seem the same but that is not the case. Blended learning focuses on the combination between offline and online learning, whereas hybrid learning is about finding the right mix for you out of all the possibilities in learning, no matter if they are offline or online."[15]
- Micro-modules: "… a way of teaching and delivering content to students in small and very specific bursts that is used to support blended learning and encourage teacher-student discussion in flipped classroom."[16]
- Problem-based learning (PBL): "… is a teaching method in which complex real-world problems are used as the vehicle to promote student learning of concepts and principles as opposed to direct presentation of facts and concepts."[17]

---

[12] Cf. Washington University, https://www.washington.edu/teaching/topics/engaging-students-in-learning/flipping-the-classroom/.

[13] Ibid.

[14] Dziuban et al. https://www.washington.edu/teaching/topics/engaging-students-in-learning/flipping-the-classroom/, under "Introduction".

[15] Driesen, https://www.anewspring.com/blended-and-hybrid-learning/.

[16] CUHK Engineering Media Studio, http://studio.erg.cuhk.edu.hk/micro-modules/about-micro-modules.

[17] Illinois CITL, https://citl.illinois.edu/citl-101/teaching-learning/resources/teaching-strategies/problem-based-learning-(pbl); Batty, pp. 243–260; Clough/Shorter, pp. 277–302.

- Experiential learning (EXL): is rather a general teaching and learning concept than a special teaching mode. EXL is based on the idea of "learning by doing" in contrast to "cognitive learning". EXL has been described as comprising four stages, i.e. concrete experience, reflection, abstract conceptualization, and active experimentation.[18]
- Clinical legal education: is as well a general legal education approach which aims to teach students "in a legal clinic where they have to deal with problems faced by real clients".[19]

9.3.3 In Particular: FCs

I had mentioned earlier[20] that I have started to flip my LIBT course about seven years ago. I do not want to go back to traditional lecturing, because I believe that the FC concept has worked very well for this course. Together with my co-author Jenny Chan I have set out my FC experience in our book "Flipped Classrooms for Legal Education".[21] I summarize the main points as follows:

For our purposes we had defined FCs as online (video or audio) lectures which allow to free in-class time for interactive exercises to foster deep learning.[22] Perceived advantages of FCs are:

- Improved learning experience and learning outcomes;
- Accommodation of different learning styles;
- Implementation of student-centered learning principles;
- Easier (online) revision;
- Increased flexibility and convenience for students who can watch online lectures when and where they wish;
- Possibility to enhance IT literacy; and
- More in-class time for interactive exercises.[23]

As mentioned earlier, it is difficult to prove that FCs really lead to improved learning outcomes.[24] However, based on the available assessment tools, we concluded that the FC concept was beneficial for the LIBT course.[25] In particular, the main reason for me to adopt the FC-concept was the possibility to free up in-class time for interactive exercises, which seemed to be particularly helpful for the topics covered by my course.

[18]Lam/Chan/Simpson/Kelly.

[19]Lewis, https://orca.cf.ac.uk/27655/1/CLINICED.pdf; cf. Rice/Coss; Combe, pp. 281–295; Owen, pp. 421–429; Ramsden/Marsh, pp. 447–459.

[20]*Supra*, 7.2.

[21]Wolff/Chan.

[22]Cf. ibid., p. 13.

[23]Cf. ibid., pp. 23–37.

[24]*Supra*, 7.2.

[25]Ibid.

The production of FCs is relatively easy. The lecture can be recorded and turned into an audio or video file. For video recording the teacher is filmed while lecturing (so-called "screen capture approach") or only the teacher's oral explanations related to each PowerPoint slide are recorded (so-called "white board approach"). The screen capture approach is technically most challenging. None of the three approaches, i.e. audio only approach, screen capture approach and white board approach, requires any complicated technological set-up or know-how, but can be easily done. Most modern laptop and desktop computers already come with the required technical features. Universities and law schools normally provide software like Echo 360, Panopto to support the recording. Furthermore, during the COVID-19 pandemic, when most of the law teaching is conducted online, ZOOM recording has become very popular and many law teachers are now familiar with this approach.[26] Again, the production is easy and cheap, if the teacher remembers that perfect recordings are neither expected by students nor are they necessary.[27]

The distribution of the online lectures can either be done through intranets, i.e. institutional online platforms such as Moodle or Blackboard. Alternatively, public channels such as YouTube, Vimeo or SoundCloud can be used for the distribution.[28]

Given the ongoing hype about the FC concept one must remember that law teachers have always expected students to prepare for class, and FCs are based on this very idea. The Socratic Method,[29] as it is used in many North-American law schools, comes very close to the FC notion when knowledge and skills, which students have acquired outside the classroom, are re-enforced during in-class Q&A sessions. The FC concept (only) differs in that it does not require students to prepare for class in the library, but by watching online lectures.[30]

9.3.4 Co-teaching

Co-teaching[31] is sometimes the deliberate choice of teachers. More often it is a matter of teaching allocation needs and individual teachers may not even be consulted. I have co-taught courses with colleagues whom I knew, and it did not matter that their teaching style was completely different from mine. Students seemingly enjoyed the variety. On another occasion I was given the option to co-teach with a colleague or to teach the whole course on my own without teaching credit or extra compensation for the additional hours. I opted for the latter. I did so because I was simply not sure if it would be enjoyable for us to co-teach, as our personalities were rather different and we even had different opinions regarding the contents on which we should focus.

---

[26] Also cf. Draper/Gibbon/Thomas, pp. 316–334.

[27] Wolff/Chan, p. 67.

[28] Ibid., pp. 93–94.

[29] Cf. *supra*, 7.8.

[30] Wolff/Chan, pp. 47–48.

[31] Cf. Caplow/Fullerton, pp. 103–127; Villa/Thousand/Nevin.

Co-teaching requires coordination, which can lead to challenges. I once met one of my co-teachers in the corridor with another colleague. He jokingly asked me if I was well prepared for the lecture about 15 min later. I replied that this was indeed a very good joke because on that day it was surely his turn to teach, a suggestion which he immediately rebutted. While we were both laughing, the other colleague was already rolling her eyes as she was the only one who understood the seriousness of the situation. She sent me straight to my office where I had to discover that it was indeed my turn. I used the remaining 10 min to collect my lecture notes which luckily I had prepared two months earlier and to photocopy the question papers for the students to be used in class. To cut the story short, I survived. When I tried to make fun of myself at the end of that class by explaining that for the first time in my life I had just delivered three hours of ad hoc shooting from the hip, students were unable to understand. I figured that for them it was just unimaginable that a professor still had to prepare for class. Interesting, but completely wrong!

On another occasion we had four different colleagues involved in the delivery of a core common law course. Three colleagues happily followed the script prepared by the course leader which had been tried and tested for years. The fourth colleague preferred to teach all his courses in a very idiosyncratic way. The course leader stayed calm throughout the term. However, when it came to setting exams, things were about to hit the fan, because that fourth colleague had taken a very different teaching approach, apparently focused on different themes and according to rumors not discussed a single case. Nonetheless, he refused to draft a separate exam paper for his students. I do not remember how the issue was settled. But this example shows that co-teaching can lead to special issues.

The previous paragraphs seem to suggest that co-teaching should better be avoided. But I do not want to give this impression. Co-teaching can be very rewarding, inspiring, free synergies and have all those other advantages that human-to-human interaction and collaboration can generate for the benefits of the students. But human-to-human interaction and collaboration can of course also end up in disaster.

9.3.5 Guest Lecturers

It can be extremely useful to invite guest lecturers to take over certain teaching sessions or parts of it. For example, visitors from other institutions can add color and variety. Practitioners can bring their viewpoint to the classroom not just because of what they have to say, but also because of the different (professional!) way how they present themselves. But inviting outsiders to teach also carries risks.

First, it is for each institution to determine how much of a law course can be delegated to outside third parties, if special procedural requirements such as obtaining prior approval are required and what governance and quality control measures are to be adopted. While guest lectures can be extremely helpful, it is in the first place the teacher who is tasked to deliver the course.

Second, as already mentioned above,[32] teaching does not come natural to everybody and a successful lawyer is not necessarily also a good teacher. Personally, I think this does not matter too much if the involvement of a practitioner in the course delivery is limited. Students do probably learn more from the way the guest lecturer presents herself than from the form and the contents of the presentation. However, guest lectures that qualify as bad teaching should of course be kept to a minimum. While governance and quality control are normally a matter for the institution, it is also for the inviting teacher to take the necessary steps.

Third, guest lectures must fit into the course structure. A friend who passes through town and not only happens to be a partner with an international law firm but would also be happy to teach a class in her area of expertise, may be a great visitor. It is a different question if the friend is also able and willing to teach the subject matter which according to the course outline is to be taught exactly on the day of visit and at the same level as the course is normally taught. In many cases it will be more suitable to organize a seminar or talk outside the regular teaching time.

9.3.6 Distance Law Learning[33]

Distance learning courses can be delivered in very different ways. In the old days, teaching and learning materials that were sent back and forth between the students and teachers or the institution via mail sometimes supplemented by block-teaching modules. During the COVID-19 pandemic, distance learning in the cloud became the new normal and law schools around the world have come to appreciate this new approach. Neither teachers nor students must be physically present on campus or any other place.[34] In fact, they can teach and learn in locations far away from each other as long as internet is available. Distance learning is relatively cheap,[35] it allows for more flexible law learning approaches[36] and ultimately a physical campus may no longer be necessary.

Three main concerns overshadow distance learning practices. First, the teacher personality[37] may not come across in the same way as in face-to-face in-class teaching. It is therefore questionable if learning outcomes can be achieved through distance learning at the level of courses that are taught in the "normal" in-class mode.[38] Certainly online teaching requires a different pedagogical approach. Most law teachers to whom I have spoken were rather vehemently opposed to any form of law teaching other than the face-to-face in-class approach and I agreed to these

[32] *Supra*, Chap. 2.

[33] Cf. Bennett, pp. 1–15.

[34] Ibid., p. 7.

[35] Ibid., p. 6.

[36] Ibid.

[37] Cf. *supra*, 7.5.

[38] Also cf. Jones/Rajvinder/Lucassen, pp. 49–69.

views. However, I think that most of us had not been involved in any distance learning before. The COVID-19 outbreak has changed this and forced us to fundamentally rethink.

The second issue of concern is governance and quality control. For example, it is difficult to ensure that students of an online course or those who take an online examination are the ones who have signed up.[39] How to deal with class-participation issues?

Third, interactivity[40] between teacher and students is possible, provided that the online system allows this. However, such interactivity is still of a different quality as compared with face-to-face in-class interactivity and may again require a different pedagogical approach.

This is not the place to expand the discussion on the online teaching experience during the COVID-19 pandemic. Many research projects have been initiated to explore related aspects and will hopefully soon provide comprehensive and reliable information regarding the dos and don'ts. I personally have come to appreciate the advantages of online teaching. Furthermore, because of globalization, the increasing need of law schools to generate additional funding and—most importantly—the travel restrictions imposed as a result of the COVID-19 outbreak, distance learning will certainly gain further importance. This would also be in line with the developments in legal practice where increasingly face-to-face interaction is replaced by online alternatives. Eventually, the viability of any distance learning option will depend on the questions if learning outcomes[41] can be achieved and if quality control can be ensured like in face-to-face in-class teaching settings. COVID-19 seems to have forced law schools around the world to acknowledge that this is indeed possible.

9.3.7 Communicating the Teaching Mode

Some years ago, our university had started to promote the use of micro-modules.[42] One of my colleagues was a little concerned about this new teaching tool, but he did what was expected and produced micro-modules for his course. As he put it, he "made a big fuss about it" in class so that students would understand this new teaching and learning approach. The course went well, students used the micro-modules to deepen their understanding of certain topics and the colleague's teaching evaluations went up. Great! All the worries that the micro-modules may not work had fortunately proved to be wrong.

In the following year, the very same colleague used his micro-modules again. Since they had worked so well in the year before, he did no longer see the need to talk about them in class. He just focused on his teaching, which—although he would

[39]Cf. Hemming, pp. 283–308.

[40]Cf. *infra*, 9.4.

[41]Cf. *supra*, 3.3.

[42]Cf. *supra*, 9.3.

not admit this—was superb as in previous years. Surprisingly teaching evaluations were down this year with no comments about the micro-modules.[43]

This story and similar reports from other teachers are important. They confirm that the way a course is taught should be communicated pro-actively to students. We need to explain that we teach in a particular way and why, what the advantages are and probably even how much work it took to prepare for class. In contrast, failure to share information about the teaching mode with students may lead to misunderstandings. In the worst case students may even feel ambushed.

9.4 In Particular: In-Class Interactivity

I am promoting in-class interactivity throughout this book.[44] In short, in-class interactivity means that it is not just the teacher who delivers contents and teaches skills to the student, but that in-class sessions comprise teacher-student and/or student-student exchanges with the goal to foster deep learning outcomes.[45] There are many different ways how in-class interactivity can be achieved and again I am touching upon many related aspects in other parts of this book. Here are some additional thoughts and observations:

First, traditionally interactive teaching has been reserved for small group teaching sessions. My experience shows that the underlying conventional wisdom is not at all correct. Large group teaching does not prevent in-class interactivity, although some adjustments or compromises may be necessary.[46] Second, as in relation to other teaching approaches, it is important to communicate the advantages of in-class interactivity to students in very clear terms. Repetition does not do any harm.[47] Third, in-class interactivity normally takes the form of Q&A or some form of exercise. As far as contents are concerned, three different approaches are possible:

- In-class interactivity can relate to substantive knowledge and skills covered in earlier teaching sessions. Take the example of 15–20-minute Q&A modules regarding topics covered in previous weeks' classes. The main goal of this kind of in-class interactivity is repetition and internalization.
- In-class interactivity can also relate to contents and skills students have acquired outside the classroom in preparation of the in-class session. For example, the Socratic method[48] and the FC model rely on this approach.[49] Here the main goal

---

[43] Many thanks to my colleague, Alan Gibb, for his permission to report this story here.

[44] Cf. in particular *supra*, 5.3; also Whaley, p. 1390.

[45] Cf. *supra*, 7.8.

[46] *Supra*, 7.6.

[47] Cf. *infra*, 9.12.

[48] Cf. *supra*, 7.6.

[49] *Supra*, 9.3.3.

is to reinforce the acquisition and internalization of knowledge and skills covered in that teaching session.

- In-class interactivity can also relate to knowledge and skills not previously covered to support students' independent development of new knowledge and skills through the in-class interactivity. This approach is the most effective one from the deep learning[50] perspective, but it is also most time-consuming.

In discussions with other law teachers I often feel reluctance to change from the traditional lecture to interactive teaching modes. This reluctance may partly be caused by the natural skepticism vis-à-vis the unknown. In particular, in-class interactivity in big classes seems to force teachers into *terra incognita*. As mentioned above, my experience is that in-class interactivity works very well in big classes and that there is consequently no need to worry. Another reason for the reluctance to give up the lecture mode may be that the change to in-class inter-activity appears work-intensive and that contents and materials which had been used for the lecture-mode delivery have to be abandoned. In my experience also this assumption does not hold water. In-class Q&A sessions, discussions and exercises do indeed require preparation and thus additional work. However, existing materials and contents can of course be used when recapitulating the background and presenting model solutions. In fact, when I switched to the FC model, I designed in-class exercises along my existing lecture contents and materials which I was consequently able to use in class as before.

As mentioned, in-class interactivity can be achieved in very different ways. Here is a summary of some of the approaches that have worked for me:

- Discussion—the obviously easiest way of creating in-class interactivity is for the teacher to start a discussion with students. In fact, even when I am using the lecture mode, I am in constant discussions with my students which I normally start by simply raising questions related to the covered legal topics.
- Past examination questions—the use of past examination questions as in-class exercises is normally well received by students as they can learn about and benchmark their knowledge against exam standards.
- MCQs—I often use one-pagers with three to five multiple choice questions at the beginning of my teaching sessions to start the interactive discussion and thus to warm everybody up.[51]
- Hypotheticals—hypotheticals are the classic form of problem-based exercises which request students to comment on legal issues related to a particular fact pattern.
- Document analysis—students can be asked to analyze and discuss real or artificial statements, newspaper articles, memos, contracts or contract clauses, defense statements, legislation, court documents, memos, or other legal documents in full or in part.
- Drafting exercises—rather than just analyzing legal documents, in-class exercises can request students to draft them. In my experiences students enjoy drafting

[50] For the notion of deep learning cf. supra, 7.8.

[51] Cf. infra, 9.10 and 10.9.11; also Fry/Crewe/Wakeford, pp. 234–242; Case/Donahue, pp. 372–387.

exercises very much, which can—as explained above[52]—be used to achieve also substantive law learning outcomes.
- Negotiation exercises—students can be asked to develop solutions for legal problems or to come up with drafts and to negotiate these with their peers. This exercise form is normally most appreciated by students.[53]

9.5 Teaching Styles

The teaching mode is the general pattern how a class is taught. This must be distinguished from a teacher's personal style, i.e. the way if and how she delivers her teaching sessions, in particular how any interaction with students takes place and whether the teacher wishes to adopt interactivity at all. The teaching style will normally at least to a certain extent determine the teaching mode, as the teaching mode reflects the teacher's personal preferences. In contrast, it appears less likely that the teaching mode affects the teaching style because the teaching style reflects the teacher personality.[54] Teacher personality is of course to a large extent also a matter the teacher's cultural background. Research shows that it takes a very long time to change cultures.[55] Having said that, a teaching style can be changed and sometimes it has to be changed. For example, when I came to Asia, I had difficulties adjusting, because students were not used to my very direct (German) way of addressing them. I have changed my approach (admittedly only slightly) to adopt to a different cultural environment.

It is rather difficult to determine which teaching style works best. First, there is again the issue if and how success can be measured.[56] Second, teachers, the students and teaching environments differ significantly, for which reason it is almost impossible to generalize. This means that it is for every law teacher to find her teaching style which is suitable given all the factors concerned. The following random observations and comments must be read in this context.

I had addressed in an earlier section the question whether toughies or softies are better teachers.[57] While I am not able to provide a final answer, I am conscious that the personality of a teacher may determine where she stands and thus which style is adopted. Again, however, the style can be changed.

According to my own experience and observations, personalized teaching is extremely helpful. What does this mean? First of all, it means that students appreciate if the teacher builds her personal stories into the delivery of a class.[58] These stories

[52]Cf. *supra*, 5.3.

[53]Ibid.

[54]Cf. *supra*, 7.5.

[55]Wolff 2018, pp. 21–24.

[56]*Supra* 7.2.

[57]*Supra*, 7.6.

[58]Also cf. Whaley, p. 1388.

can relate to the taught topic, e.g. when the teacher had to deal with the legal issue under discussion as a legal professional or in a private matter.

> Your students will be interested in you as a *person*, and, over the course of your class, you should tell them something about yourself, and particularly about your real-life legal experiences. They are hungry for such knowledge and will pay careful attention. This can lead to off-the-topic discussions that are nonetheless valuable learning tools.[59]

In fact, teacher stories do not have to be directly related to a taught topic. When I explain in my class why lawyers should avoid the use of the passive voice,[60] I always tell the story of a former girlfriend. I had the key to her flat and went there from time to time to watch TV because I did not have a telly myself. When I was once overcome by hunger while watching the news, I searched her fridge and found a chocolate bar and ate it. I left a note saying: "The chocolate has been taken." I explain to my students that I was of course joking. But by using the passive voice I was able to defer responsibility "into the unknown" and this is what the passive voice does.[61] "And now that you have heard about my former girlfriend", I continue, "you will hopefully never forget that we as lawyers have the eternal duty to fight the passive voice until it will have disappeared."

I am not promoting the idea that law teachers should conduct daily soul-striptease' in front of their students to become successful teachers. In particular, there is of course no need to talk about boyfriends, girlfriends, wives, husbands or partners. I remember one of my own former teachers who kept complaining about his wife in class and how he dealt with her attitude. While all of us found this completely inappropriate, I must admit that I will never forget this teacher and his teachings partly because of those stories he told us.

The point I am trying to make is that special personal features, good or bad, make it easier to remember things. My father was the head of a large hospital unit. I remember one Christmas a friend from the US had sent me a baseball cap as a Christmas present. After our usual Christmas dinner when my father was about to make his move to the hospital to see his patients, he asked me if he could wear the cap. I was stunned as it was surely cold outside, but my father was a very conservative 60 plus German who was working in a countryside hospital where probably hardly anybody even knew what baseball was about. My father explained with a witty smile: "You know, you always need to give your people something to talk about.", and off he was with my baseball cap. When he came back he happily reported how the hospital doorman had looked at him twice and when my father had entered the lift he saw the doorman excitedly picking up the phone to tell others what kind of Christmas surprise they were about to be exposed to.

My father's baseball cap story shows why and how personalized teaching works. You do not have to tell stories, you may have other memorable features to share. When I was a student, we had one professor who would insert a double-cough after

[59] Cf. ibid., p. 1395.

[60] Wolff 2018, p. 109.

[61] Ibid.

every third sentence. Some students found it cute, I hated it, but we all remembered him. Another example was the presenter at a seminar who constantly made sounds which were something between a pig's grunting and the roaring of a dying Mercedes. As for the general content and form of delivery the seminar was excellent, but not unforgettable had it not been for the accompanying sounds of the presenter.

Finally, I have already mentioned the judge who had delivered those entertaining and also otherwise excellent lectures at my alma mater.[62] Apart from his brilliant lecture style and contents he had another outstanding personal feature - he always wore very old-fashioned bright ties which never matched the color of his shirts. I always suspected that this was part of his show. You don't have to be cool to be an effective teacher, but you must ensure that you and your teaching are unforgettable.

9.6 Teaching Materials

When I was a student, professors would not provide any hand-outs or other teaching materials or often not even inform us about any readings to support their teaching. If we were lucky, the professor would recommend a textbook he found helpful for his (always: "his" as there were no female law professors) and a course outline. When I started to teach in Hong Kong, I was rather surprised at what was expected here. Not only do we have to provide comprehensive reading lists, but normally self-made lecture notes or online materials are expected as well. Even after 20 years of law teaching in Hong Kong, I find this a bit over the top. For example, it may be understandable that for certain courses which cover exotic subjects, proper textbooks or articles may not be available and the preparation of special teaching materials is therefore necessary. However, it seems somewhat strange to be asked to produce anything but a lecture outline in core areas, given that the library is full of books and other materials which have been published by leading experts in the field and should represent state of the art. But, as mentioned, there are institutional expectations, there are demands from the students and there is peer pressure. Sometimes it is therefore easier just to go with the flow.

What is the reason why lecture notes seem to be so important for students? First, lecture notes give the (false) impression that students do not have to record anything themselves. In fact, many law students nowadays hardly take notes during class.[63] This may be a worrying trend, because note taking is not only a good way to reinforce the learning process, but also because in their professional lives students will often be required to minute meetings etc., and without prior practice this will not be an easy task. Second, students may be fixated on lecture notes because they assume that nothing outside the lecture notes can be covered in assessments. In the past students have sometimes asked me to confirm this. I usually respond with a broad smile and explain that the lecture notes are of course meant for convenience only. They are in

62 *Supra*, 7.5.

63 Murphy/Ryan, Jr./Warnapala, pp. 2017–229.

no way meant to be comprehensive or pre-determining for the exam. Sometimes I add: “Nice try!” with another smile.

Normally lecture notes and other teaching materials which teachers produce for students are the result of a lot of hard work.[64] They may also represent special ideas of the author in terms of contents and form. Needless to say that, if you produce teaching materials, they better be good, accurate and not violate the law, in particular the copyrights of others. A very important topic in this regard is the legal and moral ownership of self-produced teaching materials.[65] What if another teacher takes over a course? In many universities the copyrights to teaching materials produced by employees are owned by the institution. While this point is well taken, proper recognition should always be given to the original author of the materials when inherited and used by another teacher.

Apart from self-produced teaching materials teachers can prescribe mandatory readings, online resources or other publications which students must study to prepare for class or for the examination. Alternatively, the teacher can provide lists of suggested readings. I prefer the latter approach at least as far as post-graduate courses are concerned. I regularly explain to students that university education is for adults and that it is the beauty of this feature that students are free to decide how they want to support their studies. I still provide lists of suggested readings which students may or may not use. Publishers are of course less happy with this approach, as mandatory books are good and sustainable business.

In one of my previous institutions I had a colleague who once had to deal with an enquiry from his students why the prescribed textbook did not cover a certain theme which he had discussed over three weeks in class. When he told us about this incident, he shrugged his shoulders with his charming smile and remarked that he could of course not know the contents of all the textbooks out there. My suggestion that, before recommending reading materials, it may make sense for a teacher to familiarize himself with what is recommended earned me another broad smile.

Can you make your own book mandatory reading for your course? Or at least suggested reading? Of course! Everybody does it and so do I.[66] In fact, the recommendation will in many cases make absolute sense because the course will most likely follow the structure and contents of the book. And still, to recommend my own book always makes me feel funny, although I do not earn a penny from additional sales. I have tried to address the situation by stressing in class that enough copies of my books are available in the library and that there is not real need to buy it. Some students still buy my books, but I suspect that the majority is just photocopying them because the publisher has made them really expensive. I also always announce in class that extensive photocopying is illegal and constitutes theft of intellectual property. Students do not seem to worry too much. I have seen complete copies of my books on students’ desks in the classroom. In these situations, I explain again that unauthorized extensive copying is illegal, that I could confiscate the copy, but will

[64]Cf. Johnstone.

[65]Cf. Alexandra/Miller, pp. 87–96; Gadd/Weedon, pp. 3231–3250.

[66]Cf. Whaley, p. 1431.

not do so on the understanding that I will never see an illegal copy again in class. My approach does not really work, I admit. But at least I have given it a try.

A lot of teaching materials are nowadays available online. This includes books and articles, but also very useful audio and video recordings. The problem with these so-called open educational resources (OER) is that they often do not cover exactly what is needed for a particular course, requiring either the course to be adjusted or acceptance of the shortfall.[67]

9.7 Course Settings

The physical settings of law courses can differ significantly. Law teachers normally do not have much choice but must accept decisions which are made by administrators with regard to financial viability, time tabling and availability of resources. Attempts to get the setting changed requires efforts which are often enough in vain, simply because of the famous "circumstances in each case". Nonetheless, it may be worth a try if what has been prescribed does not match the intended course delivery mode. This section briefly highlights three important features of the many different aspects related to course settings.

First, the teaching time is important for any course. Everybody knows that Monday mornings and Friday evenings are killers for both students and teachers. Saturdays are better, at least in Hong Kong, although it remains unclear why. And again, often there is not much that can be done about the assigned teaching slots, as time tabling is an extremely complex issue which needs to take into account many different factors, most of them not being changeable.

Second, the teaching venue can be crucial for the success of a course. Take the example of my LIBT course again. As explained, I have adopted a teaching mode which aims at substantive law learning through skills training.[68] My course always comprises between 60 and 80 students and administrative colleagues therefore normally arrange for my course to be held in a lecture theatre that can host up to 90 students with fixed desks and benches. This setting is not perfect, as many of my in-class exercises require group work. However, I still manage by gathering groups in different corners of the venue. It is inconvenient, but not to the extent that there is a need to consider or even fight for an alternative.

There are of course other reasons why a teaching venue can be unsuitable. It could e.g. be too small, too far away, too noisy, too hot or too cold etc. Any course planning must consider this as well as special needs in terms of students, teacher and the course delivery as such may lead to special requests sent to those in charge of room allocation.

Small class teaching versus big class teaching is an aspect to be considered not just in the context of the allocation of the teaching venue. The OxCam small class teaching

[67] Cf. Wolff/Chan, pp. 76–79.

[68] *Supra*, 5.3.

model has become something like the global gold standard in legal education. Even ranking agencies assess the student-teacher ratio and assign marks accordingly. The assumption is that small is beautiful and big is ugly. But, do we really need small class teaching? Do we have hard evidence confirming that small class teaching leads to better learning outcomes?

The first proper law course I ever taught was the one on "Private Law for Non-law Students", which I had mentioned in an earlier chapter.[69] The course took place on a Monday morning at 8:15am in a lecture theatre which was so large that I could hardly see the faces in the backrows. Nevertheless, I was in constant conversation with my 500 plus students, the course was always packed, and the feedback I got was great.[70] I loved it! I mention this not only because I was happy to be a star, but also because I want to challenge the assumption that small-class teaching is necessary at all cost. I acknowledge that it would be very difficult to do laboratory teaching for 500 students. But, is small-class teaching otherwise really always a must? In particular when you teach law? Small-class teaching may even be harmful when it gives students the wrong feeling that they are being taken care of and that class attendance is sufficient to achieve learning outcomes.[71]

Third, a few words about teaching equipment. A lot of hi-tech tools and facilities are nowadays available in law schools or can be easily obtained via the internet. In addition, teachers have their own favored tools, starting with the use of white or black boards and PowerPoints to the establishment of sophisticated course platforms or other online tools. I often wonder if all these tools are really all that useful. My suspicion is that sometimes they are just toys or attempts to beautify courses which are not beautiful at all. However, I may be completely wrong and even biased because my generation tends to prefer the whiteboard over online gimmicks.

I use PowerPoints in class, I use FCs[72] and I use my University's teaching platform Blackboard. Most recently the COVID-19 pandemic has forced ZOOM upon us as means to conduct classes online. Most colleagues will agree that it was a pleasant surprise how well it worked. Having said that, the first thing I do when preparing my Blackboard site for a new class is to de-activate the feedback function. First, I simply do not have time to constantly monitor student comments online. Second, I know how difficult it is to come up with precise answers in writing, which in any event may trigger an avalanche of follow-up questions that are probably caused by the desire to engage the professor rather than to discuss a legal issue. Finally, I always announce in the first teaching session of each of my courses that I am happy to meet and talk to all my students about any kind of issue they may have, during office hours. However, questions related to the form or substance of my class must be asked in class "because other students also want to benefit from your excellent contributions." My approach may not be in line with the notion of student centeredness of modern

---

[69] *Supra*, 7.6.

[70] Ibid.

[71] *Supra*, 7.8.

[72] *Supra*, 9.3.3.

legal education.[73] I also know that other colleagues do things very differently. But my approach has worked very well for me and my students so far.

9.8 Teaching Outfit

I always teach in a suit and I am wearing a tie. In recent years I have, however, considered adopting the Silicon Valley style, i.e. to wear suits, white or blue shirts, sneakers, but no tie. I have only considered this! I really like my suits and my ties.

When I started teaching law in Hong Kong, I came from private practice. I was used to wearing suits and ties and I continued to do so when I took up my new position. I did so although wearing suits and ties is often no fun in Hong Kong. For about six to seven months of the year it is boiling hot with humidity levels of up to 99%. We are used to seeing people who have sweat their shirts and even their suits through and through. And we are used to this happening to ourselves. It is difficult for me to explain why I continue to teach in suits and why I even wear ties. Maybe it is just part of my approach to work. Probably I also do it out of respect for my students. And maybe, in a way at least in my first years of teaching my formal attire gave me some protection in the sense that at least from the dress code point of view nobody could challenge me.

The dress style of law teachers is normally more conservative than in other disciplines. Students certainly monitor their teachers' attire. I had mentioned earlier the famous judge whose lectures were always packed with students due to his ability to be informative and entertaining at the same time.[74] As also mentioned, his outfit was outrageous to the extent that everybody thought that this was an intentional part of his show. The dress code is a strategic issue for one university which for years ran a booth at one of the South-East Asian education fairs. Every university member was dressed completely in black and colleagues from that university confirmed to me that the dress code was prescribed by the institution.

Some years ago, I heard about an article according to which a formal outfit increases the chances of better teaching evaluations. Interesting stuff, although I was not able to locate the article. What is certainly true is that through the way they present themselves law teachers—like any other person—create an image of themselves. They determine how they are perceived by students and by others. The teaching outfit is part of this.

As a baseline teaching outfit must be respectful. This also implies that the chosen clothing style must be in line with local culture and customs which may differ. It is important to find out about no-goes, although I have absolutely no idea where e.g. crocs stand in this regard. There may also be an institutional culture, but it is a different story if you wish to comply or you make that famous point about academic freedom. I personally try to adhere to my own style. This is not because I think that my

---

[73] Cf. *supra*, 7.9 and *infra*, 10.8.

[74] *Supra*, 7.5.

suits and ties look professional and that we are teaching a professional subject. More importantly, I trust that—subject to the basics which I have just outlined—everybody should wear what she or he feels most comfortable with.

Tattoos have become very fashionable in recent years. I read that that one out of five Germans is tattooed. Different cultures may have different perceptions of tattoos. In some countries certain types of tattoos may be unacceptable or even forbidden. Buddha tattoos in Thailand and Nazi emblems in Germany are examples.[75] It is important to keep this in mind when insisting on one's own right of expression.

9.9 Structured Teaching

Proper structuring of teaching sessions is as important for successful law teaching as it is important e.g. for the design of legal documents and academic papers. Teaching sessions can of course be structured in many different ways, depending amongst other things on the topic, the level of teaching (undergraduate, postgraduate, vocational), the adopted teaching mode, the teacher's preferences and last but not least the composition of the student body. It is impossible to discuss all available options here. However, two aspects deserve special attention.

First, as discussed earlier,[76] in times of outcome-based education (OBE) law teaching should be oriented towards particular learning outcomes which determine the structure of the course and its delivery. Second, there is of course a difference between structuring the substance of a teaching session and the structuring of the delivery of a teaching session. The former concerns the legal topics to be covered and can follow e.g. what textbooks prescribe.[77] In contrast, the latter is a matter of allocating in-class time to different sub-topics and potentially also different teaching modes. This is discussed in more detail below in the context of in-class time management.[78] At this point I only wish to mention that it has always worked very well for me to divide teaching sessions into three different blocks accommodating three different teaching modes. For example, I have often started with a 15–30 min Q&A session about the topic discussed in the previous week.[79] I could feel how this helped students to reinforce their understanding of the taught subject matters and for some reason they enjoyed being quizzed a lot. Even their teaching evaluation mentioned on a regular basis that the Q&A at the beginning of each week's teaching session was a very helpful exercise. Before having adopted the FC model, I would then continue

[75] Also cf. Tapp, https://teachertapp.co.uk/can-teachers-have-tattoos/.

[76] *Supra*, 3.3.

[77] Cf. Whaley, p. 1388.

[78] *Infra*, 10.12.

[79] Cf. *supra*, 9.4.

with an interactive lecture type module. The last part of my teaching sessions was always reserved for some kind of in-class exercise.

9.10 Preparing for the Entire Class Time

When I taught one of my very first courses in Hong Kong I introduced myself and the course and then I invited every student to do the same, i.e. to introduce her- or himself and explain why they had signed up for the course. I had about forty plus students in the class and it took about ten minutes to finish this exercise. Most students complied patiently with my request. However, I remember vividly two special responses. First, one attendee explained that she was the secretary of the part-time student who had registered for the class but was unable to attend on that evening due to a business meeting. She was therefore not able to give any further background information. This got her a good laugh and the very unexperienced me joined in with a nervous smile as I had no idea how to handle the situation.

Another student politely introduced herself and the motives why she had registered for the course. She finished with the words "... and I have never been asked in any of my university classes to introduce myself and to explain why I had registered for the course." I thanked her and replied that I was genuinely interested in my students' background. When I started my teaching, I could feel some tension in the classroom, and it took some time for it to disappear.

What had happened? My class was delivered in the evenings. Half of the students were part-timers and thus rather mature. As a newcomer I had considered how I would win students over and decided to use the mutual introduction to build trust and to create a nice atmosphere. Maybe I also wanted to hear that the course topic, which was a bit new in those days, was interesting thus getting some reward upfront for the hard work that I had put into the preparations. What I had not considered was that students were paying for the course. And they were paying in order to take something home. They were certainly not interested in listening to their classmates' introductions. They wanted me to deliver what they had signed up for rather than wasting time on what looked like an obvious attempt on my part to kill time during which I would not have to teach. As mentioned, killing time had not at all been my intention. But my approach was naive. Students do not like teachers because they are nice, but because they teach well and because they use all in-class time for this purpose.

Attempts to use all sorts of tricks to shorten the actual teaching time and thus the need to prepare are not all that rare. I have witnessed many (stupid) attempts of this kind. I once took an Italian language course in Rome. Much to the surprise of me and my classmates the course teacher was suddenly replaced in the middle of the two-week course. The new course teacher requested all of us for half an hour to introduce ourselves to him again, something we had already done for the first one. I also need to explain that the level of this course was rather advanced and everybody in the classroom just wanted to get trained up in sophisticated Italian grammar issues. Apparently, the teachers had other motives.

As a student in Germany I had a law professor who would always start his lectures by talking about the interesting stories that he had read in the newspaper in the morning. On other days he would talk about the things he had done the day before. Talking about news and their legal implications as well as telling the professor's personal stories can be very powerful tools to teach law. I have mentioned this in an earlier section.[80] But, students are not stupid!

We had another professor, who only taught a particular course for two thirds of the term and cancelled the rest of the classes claiming that everything that had to be covered had been taught. Even as a student I wondered how this professor got away with this. If he really thought that he had explained everything, he could have added comparative elements or in-class exercises related to the course topic for the final examination.

Sometimes it is indeed challenging to fill all the teaching time. In Hong Kong, all our postgraduate courses are taught in three-hour sessions with a break of 10–15 min in the middle. After having taught a course repeatedly a teacher normally has more material than she is able to cover. However, in particular, if a teacher teaches a course for the first time it may be challenging to assess how much substance can be delivered and how to fill exactly three hours. In this regard, again preparation is key! It is always possible to dig deeper and find more information that can be presented in class.

Sometimes there is of course simply not enough time to prepare additional substantive content to deliver in class. In this case, finishing earlier or even cancelling the classes should not be and in fact does not have to be the solution. Exercises are not only important to foster deep learning,[81] exercises also take up a lot of time.[82] Therefore, if there is spare in-class time to fill, exercises are a perfect way to do so. Very simple MCQs covering the themes addressed in that or previous teaching sessions can do the trick.[83] They can provide ample opportunity to discuss and deepen particular aspects. In addition, exercises can be helpful in emergency situations, e.g. when a teacher stands in front of the class with lots of time left. These situations are not as uncommon as one would think, especially for newcomers. Again, rather than sending students home, the remaining time should be filled with substance. And for this one should be prepared. An experienced teacher would have no difficulties to engage in Q&A with students covering any of the topics taught so far or guiding students into the topics to be covered in the sessions to come. For most of my teaching for each teaching session I have one additional exercise in form of a question paper ready for use in such situations. I try to keep this paper rather general, e.g. by addressing questions relating to the overall course topic, to allow for use throughout the whole course. Do you really need such a fall back option? Certainly not if each session

---

[80] *Supra*, 7.5.

[81] *Supra*, 7.8.

[82] I am discussing in-class exercises in various other chapters, cf. e.g. 9.4.

[83] Cf. *supra*, 9.4 and *infra*, 10.9.11.

is carefully planned. But one never knows how a teaching session goes. And it is important not to forget how it feels (or may feel) to stand in front of the class having said what was planned to be said without anything left to fill the remaining time.

9.11 Teaching Assistants

Teaching assistants (TAs) can be extremely helpful. TAs can support the law teacher not just in terms of preparing for class, but also during and after class. In particular, they can deal with administrative issues, they can take care of logistics, and they can even take over certain teaching tasks themselves if this is allowed within the governing framework.[84] Whether and how one should use TAs is a matter of personal style.

Jenny Chan, my co-author of the book on FCs who is mentioned in the first footnote of many of my articles did a wonderful job in helping me to flip my LIBT lectures.[85] She organized and set up the equipment, she was a critical listener during the recordings of my online lectures and she uploaded the recorded lectures so that I could use my in-class time for interactive exercises. But, I have never asked Jenny to prepare my online lectures or the in-class sessions or even to deliver them.[86] In fact, I have hardly ever used materials prepared by someone else. When I had to take over a course from a colleague, I consulted the available teaching materials, if any, but I have always re-written the whole course from scratch. Always!

Again, I am talking about my own approach. It is of course tempting to appoint TAs to write up lectures at least in the sense that they prepare a script which may in fact save the teacher a lot of time. And it may be a great exercise for the TA. And yet, I have never done this, and I am glad that I never did. When you stand in the classroom you need to know your stuff. Preparing the teaching session yourself is probably the most effective way of understanding what you are going to talk about and that you can present the topic(s) in the way that suits you and your students. While preparing for class you (re-)familiarize yourself with the topics, you work on aspects which you feel are not yet absolutely under control, you structure your teaching, you prepare questions and exercises and you consider how all this may work out from the students' point of view. After you have gone through this admittedly cumbersome process, you will certainly be ready for class. There is of course always something the teacher had not planned for. An unexpected question, a student who decides to be uncooperative, a venue that turns out to be unsuitable and so on. But, with proper preparations at least what is controllable is under control. Working hard for your class will also lead to a sense of ownership. As a result, a teacher will—at least to a certain extent—be passionate about her teaching. No need to say that students

[84] Cf. *supra*, 7.4.

[85] For the FC concept see *supra*, 9.3.3.

[86] Also cf. Prosser, p. 261.

will in return reward the teacher with respect, admiration, and appropriate teaching evaluations. All this may of course also work out if a TA has done the preparations. It may, but it also may not.

9.12 Marketing and Teaching

When I was still practicing, one of the most important office slogans was: "Do good things and talk about them!" Self-marketing as part of business development is indeed a very important feature of the legal world. But, how about law teachers? Do we have to engage in business development? Do we have to regard our teaching as a "product" which we have to "market" to our students?

When I talk about marketing, educational products and business development in my university, fifty percent of my colleagues would like to fire me right away. Admittedly this kind of language did not seem to match the noble ideals of academia until not long ago. But the situation may have changed. Legal Education is big business in many parts of the world.[87] Furthermore, in those famous University meetings I use related terminology intentionally. Drastic words provoke drastic reactions which will in turn hopefully instigate a discussion, eventually leading to a constant process of reflection and reconsideration which—I trust—is necessary to progress.

Even though there are nowadays many similarities between the normal business world and the education industry, there is of course no need to use terms like "marketing" and "educational products" in academia. But maybe "positive communication" about law teaching has certain benefits?

Why should we communicate about our teaching? Can we not just sit back and wait for students to attend our classes and assume that the university management will acknowledge how wonderful we are? We can give this a try. But there is no harm in reinforcement!

First, sometimes we are competing for students. We are competing internally, and we are competing externally with other institutions! During my first years of teaching in Hong Kong my law school once organized an information session for students in relation to electives for Master students. Teachers were invited to give a short introduction of their courses followed by a Q&A session. After four other much more senior colleagues had introduced their courses it was my turn. I had newly created my LIBT course and nobody had a real idea what it was about. So, I got up and said something like:

> "The course I am going to teach next term is the course on 'The Law of Cross-border Business Transactions'. My course is new and my course is special for one particular reason. My course is special … because it covers the most interesting topic you can think of and you as students will learn things which you will never ever forget throughout your entire professional careers. Detailed themes that I will cover are: …".

[87]Cf. Wu, p. 18 ("business model' of legal education"); Rist/Brand.

Actually, it did not really matter what my course was about, I already had the attention from all the students present and from colleagues in the room who looked at me in disbelief and were only slightly amused. My course was heavily oversubscribed and has been a success story ever since.

So, when you create new courses or programmes, you need to make yourself and your course or programme known. There are different ways to do that. For me it has always worked to explain why I thought that my course was the best. Yes, I always say “the best”, I do this with a broad smile, and everybody understands … that I really mean it, which is the best selling point I can have.

Do core courses require positive communication as well? All core courses are normally mandatory and will obviously find their students anyway. And yet, there is nothing wrong with being positive about the good things the teacher and students are doing. Not least, it allows for re-assurance of all concerned parties that we are doing the right thing.

How about in-class teaching? Does it make sense to explain to existing students how special the class is which they are attending?[88] What effect does it have if we tell our students that we feel great about our course, that we feel great about our students and that we feel great about how and what they learn? Why not giving students the feeling that they are part of something great? The most important outcome of this kind of positive communication is not that our teaching evaluations may go up, but rather that it may give students a sense of belonging. It will improve their appreciation of what we as teachers are doing, what they are contributing and what everybody is able to take home. All this of course is based on the assumption that the course is really good, and that teacher and students are enjoying it. I understand that this may not necessarily always be the case.

I trust that positive communication about our teaching is also helpful vis-à-vis our institution. This sounds natural when we teach a great new course or if we establish a successful new programme. But even if our course or programme is not new, why not confirming when appropriate that we are enthusiastic about what we are doing, that we have the crème de la crème of the students and that the very good exam results show how successful the course is? To avoid any misunderstandings, I am not in favor of extensive self-marketing. At the same time, it must be remembered that positive communication always helps to strengthen the brand of the law teacher herself and the brand of the law school and the brand of the university.

At one point of my teaching career I had joined an institution which was regarded as second tier. I only found out about this after I had already joined, but honestly did not really mind. However, within the school there was one programme which the programme director and those who taught on that programme praised as a top-notch elite course of study. The message was repeated over and over again. I must admit that the indoctrination worked on me and I remained brain-washed for quite some time. I realized only much later that the program was very good, but really not a class by itself. I have to smile about myself when thinking back, but this experience showed me what positive communication can achieve.

[88] Cf. *supra*, 9.3.7.

Finally, our teaching excellence should of course also be made known to third parties, i.e. by parties outside our law school and outside our university. This will entice more students to join, it may lead to support from the community and it will at least inform the world where the real stars of legal education can be found.

In case you may wonder, I really mean it!

Chapter 10
The In-Class Teaching Experience

10.1 General

My first law teaching experience took place in Beijing in winter 1988. I was working at Peking University on my PhD thesis on the then rather new Chinese labor contract system. I was very lucky that Professor Jia Junling was assigned to be my academic mentor. She did not only provide invaluable input on my research, but also allowed me to take 10–20 min of her undergraduate labor law class to introduce how German labor law addressed the weekly topic which she covered from the viewpoint of Chinese labor law. It was freezing cold in the lecture theatre and everybody was wearing at least three layers of clothes under thick down overcoats. I had never lectured before and everything was done in Chinese. I suspect that not much that I tried to explain was really understood by the audience. Anyway, it was a fantastic experience for me and I am eternally grateful to Professor Jia.

I started to teach on a more regular basis at my alma mater while working on my second PhD,[1] the so-called "Habilitation", which was a precondition to become a full professor in Germany.[2] German professors normally have one or more assistants who teach tutorials in the professor's core area, i.e. private law, public law or criminal law and I was one of those. Except for a rough lecture outline prepared by the professor teaching the main class in private law, the assistants did not receive any instructions as to how to prepare or teach the tutorials.

At my current university, the Center for Learning Advancement and Research (CLEAR) offers amongst other things courses and seminars to teachers from all faculties on all sorts of teaching and learning (T&L) related topics. Teachers can also contact CLEAR with queries and proposals. At faculty level our Associate Dean

[1]"Dr. iur. habil."

[2]For the relaxation of the requirements in recent years, cf. German Ministry of Education and Research, https://www.research-in-germany.org/en/jobs-and-careers/info-for-postdocs-and-junior-researchers/career-paths/path-to-professorship.html.

© The Author(s), under exclusive license to Springer Nature Singapore Pte Ltd. 2021

L.-C. Wolff, *The Art of Law Teaching*, SpringerBriefs in Law,
https://doi.org/10.1007/978-981-15-9148-8_10

(T&L) organizes on a regular basis law-specific teaching and learning seminars. My university and my faculty also support related research projects with generous grants. We even have a special course taught by and for our research students covering various aspects of legal education. Again, when I started my teaching career nothing like that was available. We were just thrown into teaching and were expected to perform.

This section is not about institutional teaching support. This section is rather about the in-class teaching experience of law teachers. I am trying to highlight key points with reference to my own experience which in the beginning was really learning by doing and sometimes rather painful.

10.2 The Stress Factor

For the first ten years of my law teaching career admin colleagues knew that for at least the last two hours prior to my classes they should better leave me alone as I would be very difficult to deal with. I knew this all too well and I therefore tried to stay away from people during the pre-teaching session time. The reason was very simple: I was stressed. I knew that I had to know my stuff, I had to capture the audience's attention for the entire teaching time and that if it worked out, I would be rewarded with that great feeling of satisfaction which had made me want to become a law teacher in the first place. Probably more importantly, I also knew that I would feel terrible for a couple of days if a class went wrong.

There maybe those naturally born teachers who do not feel any pressure before they go to class. I am not one of them! I know about other colleagues who feel the same. The question we need to ask is if there is something wrong in reaching those stress levels? Do we have to do more Yoga or drink more green tea? Having considered this issue for some years, my conclusion is that this is certainly not the case.[3]

Interestingly, colleagues whom students rate as their best teachers are often the ones who are most stressed about their classes. The stress level keeps us on our toes and ensures that we stay focused. In fact, the stress a teacher encounters is not a negative, destructive one. In contrast, it is at least partly caused by the excitement of getting something across to the students and every week again and again it is the question if it will work. In this regard it is also important that if the teacher is well-prepared for class,[4] once she is standing in front of her students, self-confidence kicks in and the stress is pushed aside by action. At least, that is how it works for me.

[3]Cf. however, Guthrie, pp. 5–18.

[4]*Supra*, 7.5.

10.3 Speaking Freely versus Reading Out

When I have to present conference papers and am—as it is nowadays unfortunately often the case—given only a very tight speaking time, I sometimes write out my entire presentation. Of course, when I speak, I do not just read from the manuscript. But the audience can see that I have prepared something which will allow me to finish exactly when the time is up. This never seemed to be a problem. On the contrary!

When I first started teaching in Hong Kong in Mandarin, I had written up all my lectures. Word for word! I even did mock lectures each week with a Chinese language teacher to ensure that my Mandarin was understandable. But again, in class I was not just reading out what I had prepared. Writing up the whole lecture was just a perfect, although extremely time-consuming way for me to prepare for class. I do admit that I have never heard of any colleague who has done the same. But for my classes in Mandarin I needed it.

Things are different with PowerPoints. The preparation of rather extensive PowerPoints with a lot of text is unfortunately rather common, although—to the best of my knowledge—it does not happen in my institution. I heard about law teachers who sometimes just read out their PowerPoints leading to a flood of student complaints. In fact, what is the point in attending classes if one just gets to hear the something which one could read much faster at home by oneself?

Extensive PowerPoints are tempting because they seem to provide that kind of re-assurance that everything will be alright in class. But this may also be a dangerous illusion. PowerPoints with more than three bullet point lines are nogoes. And reading out PowerPoints is even worse. In fact, reading out any materials should be avoided, if at all possible. Good law teachers speak freely!

There are of course exemptions from this general rule. A seminar conducted in September 2019 is very instructive in this regard. You can watch it online through the link provided in the footnote.[5] Apart from the fact that the professor is very knowledgeable and a great presenter, two points are important. First, he uses extremely wordy PowerPoints to allow the audience to appreciate the original texts, which makes of course sense in the context of his seminar topic. Second, the professor also explains this very rationale to the audience, i.e. he communicates his presentation approach. The seminar was a great success. Communication is everything![6]

10.4 Politically Correct Teaching

Politically correct teaching is important for a great variety of extremely important reasons. The difficulty is to determine what politically correct teaching really entails. Many abstract descriptions are available. They can help to get a general understanding and to categorize clear-cut cases. However, very often things are not straight forward,

[5] Ho, https://www.law.cuhk.edu.hk/app/greater-china-20190920/.

[6] *Infra*, 10.9.

because circumstances differ. This section cannot and is not intended to try to add to the discussion of political correctness. In particular, it cannot offer a definite answer as to what a law teacher can do and what not. It is as obvious as it is important that students must be treated with respect and that any form of discrimination is not acceptable.[7]

> Sometimes our students, our colleagues, and our alumni will behave badly, be irritating, let us down, say or do something we profoundly disagree with, or otherwise find multiple ways to be disagreeable. Sometimes, of course, they will delight us. But in any case they should be treated with respect.[8]

Again, how all this should work out in the teaching context depends on the situation on the ground. I wish to share some additional observations in the following.

As already mentioned above,[9] I had to change my formerly somewhat direct teaching style when I moved to Asia due to the different culture over here. There are as well political sensitivities as the following example shows.

The relationship between mainland China, Hong Kong, Macau and Taiwan is extremely instructive from the viewpoint of private international law.[10] Some years ago, after I had discussed related issues in class, I received an email from a mainland Chinese student requesting me to be more careful and to use politically more correct language. I was not amused and explained in the subsequent session that I had expressly not commented on the political situation and simply presented the official positions to set the scene for discussing related legal questions. After this class I received another email from another student, this time one from Taiwan. She complained over two pages that she felt hurt that I was not supporting Taiwan. I was again not happy. The following week I repeated that I had reported only on the official position and that we were looking at things from an objective legal point of view. No more emails arrived, but to pre-empt similar emails, I am now telling this story year after year in class before I embark on discussing the private international law issues concerned and I do this much to the amusement of my students.

Sometimes you step into the famous Fettnäpfchen[11] inadvertently. In one of my lectures about two years ago, I spotted that a male student in the back was wearing the same new wristwatch like a female student in the first row. I carelessly asked if this had any kind of meaning, only to be confronted by a harsh "No" from the backrow and icy silence from the front row. The female student even took off her wristwatch and let it slip into her bag. I was not sure what I had done, continued quickly with the lecture, and told myself to be more careful in the future when aiming at a quick laugh in class.

I had other terrible moments. Back in Germany I once teased a student about her hoarse voice and the intensive partying the night before which this seemed to

---

[7]Whaley, p. 1389.

[8]Coper, pp. 70–80.

[9]*Supra*, 9.5.

[10]Cf. Deißner.

[11]I.e. "to drop a brick or a clanger".

suggest, only to find out later that she had just gone through a family tragedy. I felt terrible, but the student accepted my apologies without hesitation and was very kind about this incident.

The problem is that jokes in class are entertaining and good for the general atmosphere. But, considering the risks involved should we not better exercise restraint? In particular, joking with and about individual students is rather risky. As teachers we have something like a joke-monopoly, while students hardly have the chance to make fun of their teachers during class, although some try. Is it therefore unfair to pick on some students to make the whole class laugh?

In-class jokes must of course never be insulting, discriminating or derogative. Otherwise every teacher must decide for herself. I will continue to do joke with students if I feel that I have built a relationship of trust and mutual respect with my students and that they can accept that even I sometimes make mistakes. I continue to pick on students for my in-class jokes. However, I try to ensure that the student can handle the situation. I sometimes even mention this explicitly:

> "Sir, you seem to be very confident. Can I therefore ask you a very tricky question which of course you don't have to answer if you don't want to ...".

I also try to allow some kind of reciprocity e.g. by making fun of myself. It has worked for me so far, but—as mentioned—I have had my moments.

10.5 Class Attendance

I had recalled above that when I was a student, I did not attend any classes for the last two years prior to the final First Legal State Examination which completed my undergraduate law education in Germany.[12] In fact, back then nobody cared whether students attended lectures or not. We had one (very famous!) professor who even announced in the first teaching session of a particular course that he would have to make his lecture very boring to bring the student number down to a workable size.

The approach in common law jurisdictions and in Asia is of course much more structured and more prescriptive with (perceived) less freedom as to whether and when students have to take courses and attend classes.[13] In many law schools in-class attendance may even contribute to the final grade obtained in a course.[14] There may also be institutional rules on class attendance, e.g. prescribing a minimum percentage of classes students must attend.

I have made my personal view clear in the previous sections. Students are adults and we should treat them as such. As a matter of principle, it should consequently be for students to decide if and when they wish to attend classes.[15] It cannot be the

[12]Cf. *supra*, 7.9.

[13]Cf. Skead et al. p. 366.

[14]Cf. *infra*, 10.6.

[15]Cf. however Skead et al. p. 364 (with further references).

task of law teachers to police or mother their students. Students must make their own decisions and they must live with the consequences. If they decide to skip classes, there may be a reason, and this should cause the teacher to re-consider the teaching approach adopted.

> "If an instructor has to take attendance I order to get the students to show up, perhaps that means the classroom experience is not worth the money the students are paying to take it. The true talents of such faux teacher should be applied elsewhere …".[16]

Absence from class will of course not come with any privileges. If class attendance is required to understand issues which will be tested in the examination, no student can claim that she did not know about it. In fact, every student is expected to attend in-class teaching sessions. If a student decides not to do so because there are better ways to study the subject, all the better! But, the responsibility for the outcome of such approach rests with the student. Having said that, what I have just outlined is what I perceive to be an ideal situation. I have presented my points to generate discussion, stand to be corrected and do under no circumstances wish to encourage anybody, in particular of course not my own students, to skip classes.

10.6 Diverse Student Groups

The student body of many law classes is nowadays often very diverse. Different student backgrounds in terms of nationality and culture, native speakers and non-native speakers, part-time and full-time students, freshmen and mature students, levels of professional education and so on are very common. This may lead to rather different student needs and it can at times be challenging to align those needs to form a coherent class. However, there are also very positive aspects of diverse student groups. Input from students with different backgrounds does potentially create awareness of diversity and can lead to very synergetic teaching environments. Because the creation of synergies requires interaction amongst students, in-class exercises are all the more important.[17]

10.7 Motivating Students

The student-centered educational approach is nowadays promoted everywhere.[18] This approach implies amongst other things that law teachers need to consider whether and how to motivate students.[19] Nobody seems to question this, and the

[16] Cf. Whaley, p. 1417.

[17] Cf. *supra*, 9.4.

[18] *Supra*, 7.9.

[19] Cf. e.g. Blaze, pp. 547–566.

development of modern teaching modes are often expressly aimed towards this goal. I have reported on my experiments with FCs above.[20] FCs are amongst other things regarded as advantageous from the motivational point of view because they meet the digital habits and needs of the current e-generation.[21]

But should it really be the task of university teachers to motivate students or should it not rather be students who wish to study a particular subject to motivate themselves? Students have (hopefully) made the deliberate decision to take up university studies. Vice versa, can a university professor not assume that students join her class because they want to learn from her? To push this idea even further, I have asked in an earlier section if it should therefore not be for students to motivate their teachers rather than the other way round.[22]

In my classes I do of course not just wait for my students to make moves. On the contrary, as I have outlined above, my teaching approach is very much aimed to engage and even entertain students. This is in fact about motivation. "Intrinsically motivated behaviors derive from the inherent satisfaction of those behaviors."[23] But again, it is important not to forget what the responsibilities in the teacher-student relationship are. Students are adults and must be treated as such. It appears to me that student-centeredness cannot mean that we are depriving ourselves and students of the possibility to do exactly this. Student-centeredness cannot mean that the goal of legal education is anything but to educate mature, critical, creative, and independent legal thinkers. It is for this reason that students should not be forced into the same passive role which they have played during their kindergarten, primary and secondary school times rather than being given the chance to take their fate into their own hands. Should tertiary legal education therefore not aspire to do better than it currently does?

10.8 Teacher-Student-Teacher Communication

Yes, there are indeed three crucial things for successful law teaching: communication, communication, communication! It is important for law teachers to explain what they teach and how, why and with which ultimate learning outcomes. This may be rather obvious, but while one should never under-estimate law students, one should also not over-estimate law teachers' ability to create transparency regarding their teaching. It is certainly beneficial to be explicit rather than to assume that students will see through teaching schemes and understand them.

I always set closed-book examinations. In contrast, students at my university are used to open-book examinations and anecdotal evidence has it that they actually prefer them. I always explain to my students that open-book examinations are dangerous because all the questions need to be challenging as it cannot be the idea

[20] *Supra*, 9.3.3.

[21] Wolff/Chan, pp. 23–30.

[22] *Supra*, 7.9.

[23] Cf. *supra*, 3.2.; Blaze, p. 549.

to ask students to simply copy answers from the books and other materials which are brought to the examination venue. In a closed-book examination I can also set questions which allow students to demonstrate what they have learned, i.e. to a certain extent students are assessed on their ability to reproduce substantive knowledge. Correct answers to these questions will get them close to the pass mark. I have never had problems with closed-book examinations provided that I have communicated this and my reasons in class clearly.

Teacher-student communication should not be one-directional. In contrast, students must be encouraged to "communicate back" to their teachers. Student feedback is important on issues which have arisen or may arise during and outside class sessions. How to achieve this? First, open communication is a matter of trust, and trust is created by explaining things as they are. Things are of course never as easy as they look, and circumstances can differ significantly. However, the point I want to make is that awareness of the importance of proper communication is the precondition for taking pro-active steps in the right direction.

At the beginning of each of my courses I announce that I am happy to talk to students about any matter they might want to bring up. Issues related to taught topics must be raised in class. However, I am there for my students to discuss all other matters, in particular career related questions. I then explain how students can reach me and that whilst I am very busy, it has always been possible to find time to meet with a student. I also make it clear that any enquiry will be treated confidentially. When I tried this approach for the first time, I was worried that I would end up in two hours of consultations with students every day. But this never happened. I get three to five students per term who seek my advice on course or career related matters and am happy to offer my views and we normally have very interesting discussions.

One final point is important: teachers must ensure that the student-teacher communication remains manageable.[24] This implies that unfocused communications back and forth with students without any realistic prospect to solve the issue in question must not be allowed. I have taken the drastic step to inform my students that I am not able to answer emails and that questions should be raised in person after or before class over the phone or in person during office hours. If communicated properly, this approach works. Students understand.

10.9 Ten Ways to Start a Teaching Session

10.9.1 General

> "Make the opening scene work for you. Think about the agenda. … The overture should make the music."[25]

---

[24]Also cf. *infra*, Chap. 14.

[25]Copeland/Griggs, pp. 97–98.

This quote from a book about cultural management applies to law teaching sessions in the same way. The tone must be set right at the beginning. A good start guarantees smooth sailing. In contrast, if the class opener goes wrong, the law teacher will struggle to get students back on track.

This section introduces ten different ways to start a teaching session. There are of course many other ways how a course could begin. This section only aims to create awareness for advantages and disadvantages again based on my own experience.

10.9.2 The Formal Start

Most law teachers would start their teaching sessions in a rather formal way with something like:

> "Good morning everybody! This is week three of our contract law course. Today we are looking into a very important issue: consideration. However, before we start I need to make some announcements regarding logistics …".

There is nothing wrong with these opening lines. But, let's face it, they are not very exciting. This approach may work for the first two or three teaching sessions of a term. But this kind of formal start will not allow you to capture any special attention or lead to excitement about what is to come in the next hour or so. Furthermore, variety is often better than monotone repetition of the same opener over and over again.

10.9.3 The Silent Start

At one point during my first year as lawyer, the senior partner summoned all the associates to the conference room and declared that everybody would have to attend a rhetoric seminar over the next weekend. We were not amused, because this just meant that the weekend was gone, and one had to behave because the big boss was there. Until today I am benefitting from that seminar and I am grateful that we were forced to do it.[26]

During the seminar we were asked to do mini presentations of 1–3 min, which the trainer would then use to discuss special aspects of presenting and communicating successfully. In one of the exercises I was very fortunate not to be the first presenter. The colleague who had volunteered to start was obviously shocked when after his first few sentences, the trainer turned to his neighbor to talk in a low voice about the afternoon arrangements. Once they had come to an agreement, he turned to the other participants to communicate the result. The presenting colleague was puzzled by the

[26] I have also otherwise learned a lot from the senior partner, Dr. Volker Triebel, who nowadays runs his own practice and will hopefully read these lines.

apparent disrespect. He first stopped his presentation, then tried to continue, but then stopped again. His face showed disbelief. When the room had calmed down, the poor presenter started to talk again. This time, two other colleagues, who understood what was going on, commenced a whispered, but vehement discussion about the odds of that weekend's football games. The presenter tried to calm them down by raising his voice, but to no avail.

The trainer had of course started the disruptions to demonstrate how you can and cannot deal with a misbehaving audience. The way to get such a situation under control is rather simple: you must face the audience and stay silent until everybody is granting you your well-deserved attention. When the disruption starts again, you must do the same, i.e. go silent and wait. This requires some coolness and a great degree of self-confidence. It feels strange to just stand there and wait. But it even worked during our seminar. For the subsequent presentations we all knew that we were supposed to be disruptive and of course we all enjoyed giving the presenting colleagues a difficult time. However, after a while the game became a bit boring and we also realized that it would be unfair and impolite to continue. As a consequence, each presenter was able to finish.

At the beginning of a teaching session students are often not immediately attentive. Of course not! They must inform their neighbors about last night's adventures, share the latest gossip and sometimes even talk about political developments and stock markets. And then there are always students who are late and need to squeeze themselves into the row, forcing others to stand up, move things to the side and free space. All this takes time.

What to do as teacher? The answer is: nothing! After you have arranged your lecture notes at the lectern and after you have started your PowerPoints (or whatever you are using) you look at the audience and you wait. And wait! In silence! And you wait more. If after some time certain students continue to talk while you already have the attention of others you may look at the noisy ones. And you wait! In silence! This can take a couple of minutes and as in the exercise at the rhetoric seminar with my former big boss, it may feel odd when you do it for the first time. But try it! Just wait in silence until the whole lecture theater has calmed down. Then you start with your very happy: "Good morning! Welcome back to our course on the law of …".

In this context there is another important rule to remember. Nobody expects a presenter to start talking before facing the audience. Therefore, while you are on your way to the lectern, as long as you arrange your materials for that day's teaching, nobody will pay attention to you. In other words, you can take your time to get ready. Then you look at the audience and you wait. You wait in silence until even the last student is paying attention.

Does this always work? Yes, it does! … at least in normal circumstances! However, neither silence nor lecturing will help if troublemakers attend your class for just that purpose, i.e. to cause trouble. Such a situation could be politically motivated as during the student movement of the 1960s in Europe when "blasting lectures" was rather common. Sometimes it can also happen simply because students enjoy seeing the teacher struggle. Fortunately, I had to deal with such a situation only once.

In Germany, applicants for professorial posts are normally invited to an "audition"[27] in the form of either a public talk on a particular academic topic or of a teaching demonstration session with students. After I had completed my "Habilitation"[28] which made me eligible to apply for professorships, I was invited by the University of Münster to such a teaching demonstration. I was asked to teach a session of the course "Law for non-law students". What I did not know was that the students of this course were (in)famous for giving teachers a hard time. Furthermore, the 300 or so students were informed upfront that different candidates for the professorship would deliver different parts of the course and students therefore had enough time to gang up for some fun. When I walked into the lecture, I could feel 300 pairs of eyes looking at me with excitement. After a brief introduction, the chairman of the selection committee took his seat amongst his six colleagues in the first row and I entered the stage. The noise level immediately rose to an almost unbearable level. I arranged my notes, took a deep breath and looked at the audience. And I waited in silence. I waited until the nervous looks from the members of the recruitment commission indicated that I should better forget about all those smart rhetoric concepts and start teaching. And so I did. Immediately rhythmic clapping started in the lower left corner of the teaching venue spreading like wildfire to the whole room within seconds. 300 students where rhythmically clapping and six professors in the front row were looking at me, three of whom even showed hints of an amused smile. Remember that for me this audition was about my future as a law professor.

I tried once again. I stopped talking and waited until the clapping did indeed stop. As soon as I started with my lecture again, the clapping was back, now, however, at an even higher volume. At this point I decided that enough was enough, that I would never get this job and that I could as well end this whole exercise with dignity. I lowered my voice and explained that the following would be very important for the examination, which was of course not true, and then I just did my lecture without paying any further attention to the audience. Things calmed down a bit after a while. There were some students in the front row who even took notes, and at one point somebody asked a question. But of course, I did not get the job and to be honest, I could not care less.

The situation was unusual in that as a one-time presenter, I had no standing at all. I was not the course leader, everybody knew that I was an applicant for a professorship and depended on the students' cooperation. I guess it was also important that the audience was made of non-law students without any real interest in the topic I was supposed to teach. And yet, situations like this can happen also in the normal course of teaching, although I fortunately never had such an experience again.

What if things get out of control? While everything depends on the circumstances, the baseline must be that teaching requires mutual respect between teachers and students. Teachers are trying their best to deliver their classes at the expected level and students can be expected to do their part. If teachers' efforts are sabotaged for

---

[27] In German these auditions are called "Vorsingen", which means to sing in front of jurors and accurately describes the situation.

[28] "Dr. iur. habil.", cf. *supra*, notes 1, 2.

whatever reason, then decisive action is required. The teacher may change to a very boring and fast lecture style as I had to at the University of Münster as just described. Alternatively, even more drastic steps can be required, such as stopping the session and leaving the venue to find a solution in cooperation with other colleagues and the law school management. There is certainly no need for law teachers to sacrifice their dignity just because somebody who is not supposed to be in the classroom has weird ideas about the purpose of teaching and learning law.

10.9.4 The Angry Start

How about the following start?

> "Good afternoon, ladies and gentlemen! Over the weekend I have marked the first half of your mid-term assignments. I am really disappointed! The instructions were clear, the task was easy, and I had given you many hints in class. Don't you ever listen? Or are you just not up to the standard? I really do not understand why you are wasting your and my time if you are not able or willing to follow clear instructions …".

Correct! This opening will not go down well. Students will feel frustrated, disappointed or just angry. Uncooperative attitudes will certainly be the outcome. In other words, the teacher's anger and aggression will provoke counter-anger and counter-aggression on the students' part.

One may argue that if the mid-term assignments are really that bad, then such kind of scolding is unavoidable for pedagogical reasons. But the opening tone sets the scene for the whole teaching session. An angry start will make it very difficult to draw students back to the law teacher's side. And there may indeed other ways to convey the message about the mid-term assignments.

10.9.5 The Smiling Start

Consider walking into your classroom, preparing your materials etc. and then facing your students with a broad smile. And while you are silently waiting for students to calm down you continue to smile at them. How would that work? Trust me, it would work very well. It would create a very pleasant atmosphere. Students may start smiling back at you. Your smile may even build up some excitement about what will come next.

Eight years ago, I was the Acting Dean and had to do the welcome speech for our freshmen. The colleague in charge of undergraduate programmes reminded me before the event: "… and, be nice to them!" I must have looked rather puzzled before I replied: "What do you mean? I am always nice!" She just gave me a knowing smile.

When doing my welcome speech, I told this story by making a lot of fun of that colleague and of myself with lots of smiles. The freshmen loved it.

I am not sure what caused my colleague to make that remark. Admittedly, as I had mentioned earlier,[29] I am tall, have no hair and I sub-consciously try to avoid too much smiling because—as one of my sisters suspects—this leads to even more wrinkles. I trust, however, that I am a genuinely nice person. I really do! However, I need to remind myself that my appearance may give a different impression and that smiling helps to break the ice.

In summer 2019 I did a presentation in Singapore. The first comment I got afterwards from one of the attendees, a practicing lawyer, was that she would not have imagined that somebody in a sharp dark suit could be so funny and entertaining. I was not too sure what to make of this. Should I reconsider my dress code or should I work harder on the contents of my talk to shift the audience's focus away from the entertainment factor? Anyway, I must admit that I liked the comment.

10.9.6 Reference to the Examination

> "Good morning everybody! Today we will talk about a topic which is extremely important in general, but also has a particular significance for your examination."

A teaching session started like this will ensure that the teacher has everybody's attention right away. It is just important not to over-use this opener or else nobody will believe it.

10.9.7 The Bored Start

Some years ago, I attended the welcome session for new law students at a sister institution. The professor who did the bit for one of the programmes explained that he had to step in for the programme director who was on conference leave. He explained that he also rather wanted to be at a conference, but somebody had to do this session and unfortunately it had fell on him.

While these welcome remarks were not made at the beginning of a teaching session, I thought that they were outrageous for reasons which apply in the same way also for regular teaching sessions. If students are given the feeling that they are a necessary evil, then they can hardly be expected to engage in their studies with enthusiasm and passion. If a teacher does not feel well on a particular day, she should not show it.[30] A teacher who does not feel like working with students in general has made the wrong career choice and should quickly look for another job.

---

[29] *Supra*, 7.6.

[30] *Supra*, 7.5.

10.9.8 *The Start with the Parcel*

A military instructor once told me the following story.

The class he was teaching was on first aid in combat situations. Since the course was for all new recruits irrespective of their educational background, students who had just graduated from high school and were used to studying were absolutely under-challenged and got easily bored. To ensure their attention, this instructor once brought a wrapped parcel to class and displayed it prominently and with lots of theatrics on a desk in front of the students. He then did his teaching session and indeed the audience stayed on alert in order not to miss the moment when the parcel issue would be revealed. The instructor finished without having even mentioned the parcel, picked it up again and left. The attendees of the session could hear his laughter and the laughter of other instructors, who had been waiting for him outside. He told me that for the remaining two weeks of the course, he was met by stern faces whenever he came to the classroom.

The display of the parcel had been successful as a device to facilitate the teaching. However, this initial success backfired when students realized that the parcel was just a bad joke at their cost. The situation got even worse when the instructor and his colleagues apparently laughed at them. It is not surprising that the teacher-student relationship was permanently damaged.

Mutual trust is key for success in the classroom. It is for this reason that express or implied promises by the teacher which are not kept later, are not a good idea. Therefore, the all too common remark by a teacher that a particular issue will be revisited later may help at a particular moment. However, it is a promise that must be kept.

10.9.9 *The Personal Start*

I have outlined above[31] how powerful personalized teaching can be. Our experience, our stories and our views add zest to the teaching session that we have cooked up for the students and thus make our teaching spicy and memorable. Personal stories also make great starts of teaching sessions. I once kicked-off a class by explaining to students how I had been to the races in Hong Kong's Happy Valley the night before. The start of the first race was displayed on a big screen—as we thought—at the opposite side of the racecourse. The horses ran and ran and finished, except that we still only got to see them on the screen, because that night was the only night of the season when the night-race took place at the other racecourse in Shatin, which is normally reserved for the Sunday races. Students had a good laugh, and we started the class in a cheerful atmosphere.

[31] *Supra*, 9.5.

10.9.10 The Professional Start

A variation of the start with a personal story is the start with a story the teacher has experienced as a professional or personal story with a legal angle. On several occasions I was able to begin my teaching sessions with something like this:

> "What you see on the screen is an email I received last night. I have of course anonymized the email and blackened out confidential parts. What do you think? How should I respond?"

In my experience, reference to ongoing transactions, cases and consultancies projects are great for teaching purposes, in particular if they relate directly to the taught topic.[32] Students just love it.

10.9.11 The Q&A Start

In previous years I started two of the thirteen sessions of my LIBT course[33] with a quick "Good morning", after which I distributed a MCQ question paper with the words: "You have ten minutes!" Since I have adopted the FC-concept,[34] the MCQs are all about the online lecture which students should have watched before class. The questions are rather simple and e.g. look like this:

Select the correct statement(s):

(1) (a) Legal work to support a BOT project can normally not be done by a single lawyer.
(b) BOO projects are greenfield projects.
(c) BTO projects are BTL projects.
(d) The difference between Build-Operate-Transfer projects and Build-Operate-Trade projects is that the former does not require external financing.
(e) BOT projects are normally conducted by investors from developed countries in developing countries.

(2) The purchaser of an overseas target company
(a) will never be liable for the target's debts.
(b) may not be liable for the target's debts.
(c) will never be liable for the target's debts in the case of an asset deal.
(d) may not be liable for the target's debts in the case of an asset deal.
(e) will never be liable for the target's debts under the host country's labor and social security law.
(f) may not be liable for the target's debts under the host country's labor and social security law.
(g) will never be liable for the target's debts in the case of a share deal.
(h) may not be liable for the target's debts in the case of a share deal
(i) will never be liable for the target's debts in the case of proper contractual arrangements.
(j) may not be liable for the target's debts in the case of proper contractual arrangements.

...

Experience shows that students enjoy the discussion of the MCQs very much. Again, proper communication is key. I always explain that the questions are meant to

---

[32] Cf. *supra*, Chap. 6.

[33] Cf. *supra*, 5.3.

[34] *Supra*, 9.3.3.

allow us to reconsider the legal issues covered in that session. They are hardly about right or wrong, because—as will be seen from the discussion—the answers depend very much on how you interpret the questions. This should, however, not prevent us from starting the discourse in the first place. It is for the same reason that I would normally not use MCQs as exam questions. The risk of misunderstandings is just too high.[35] But again, as openers they are great.

10.10 "Back Teaching"

Another important rule: never talk to your students without facing them! During class from time to time we all have to turn to white boards, PowerPoints or we have to make other arrangements which force us to turn away from our audience. Do not continue talking during those moments! Never ever!

Why not? Well, first it will obviously be difficult to hear you. Even if you raise your voice when speaking against the wall rather than to your students, your explanations may be much harder to understand, not least because they are not supported by your mimics and your gestures. Second, when you are talking while not facing your students, you do not give them attention and they will do the same to you. This is rather normal. Why would you want to communicate with somebody who is not even looking at you? Third, facing the person(s) you wish to speak to is a matter of respect and self-confidence. At the time I am writing this paragraph I am reflecting on a meeting from the day before with somebody who continued not to look at me but at the sheet of paper in front of him while biting his fingernails. This did certainly not encourage the open conversation that I would have wished for both of us.

Back to the classroom:

I must admit that I sometimes find myself "back teaching". This sometimes happens when I am running out of time. But when I realize my mistake, I immediately turn around and say something like:

> "Apologies, a teacher should never teach with the back to the students. This is impolite and leads to problems in terms of acoustics. So, let me start over again …".

And, I say this with a broad smile. Communication is everything! And communication that comes with a smile is even better.

10.11 Time Management

Time management is obviously crucial for successful law teaching. At the same time, finishing a teaching session right on time is extremely difficult for several reasons. It can happen that a teacher is carried away when lecturing about something that she

35Cf., however, also Fry/Crewe/Wakeford and Case/Donahue.

really cares about. Or the teacher may have so much content to address that it is hard not to speak faster and faster, just to realize at the end of the class that students are lost. Furthermore, while I strongly believe in in-class exercises as the best tool to achieve deep learning effects,[36] in-class exercises are especially tricky in terms of time management. Students may finish the exercise far ahead of schedule because it is too easy, or they are too good, leaving in-class time that now needs to be filled by the teacher. An exercise can also turn out to be unexpectedly difficult with additional time needed to help students to understand what it is about and to develop solutions. Moreover, students may be uncooperative, and time may be required to get them on track. In the best case the exercise is so successful that students do not want to stop working on their task. But, how to avoid overruns?

As always, good planning is important, although this as well as the implementation of the teaching plan is challenging. Experience certainly helps. In addition, here are three points which I found useful.

First, before having adopted the FC-approach,[37] I normally broke up my three-hour teaching sessions into smaller units. For example, I would schedule 30 min at the beginning for Q&A regarding topics discussed in the previous week. I have already reported that many students mentioned in their teaching evaluations that they found this kind of repetition extremely helpful.[38] I then did 60 min of inter-active lecturing which I would divide up further according to sub-topics into smaller units. I would use the remaining class time after the break to do one or two exercises. I always planned for about 10–15 min at the end as buffer or for de-briefing purposes. Of course, teaching times and formats as well as course types are very different. But time management becomes much easier when the planning is done in regard to smaller units.

Second, less is very often more!

> "One impossible goal is to teach everything. … Make peace with the idea that you will have to leave out a great deal."[39]

I had to make the rather painful experience that very often when I tried to put too much into my lectures they just did not go well. I was talking too fast, students could feel how I was rushing along and that I was stressed for fear that I would not be able to deliver what I wanted to deliver. Furthermore, since I was trying to cover too much, there was not enough time to explore issues in depth. Again, students were of course able to understand this and made corresponding comments in the teaching evaluation forms. The point is that it must be accepted that there is always something which cannot be covered. Law teaching cannot be and is not even meant to be comprehensive. Rather than focusing on all those details which nobody can remember anyway, law teaching should be about concepts, principles and skills to

---

36 *Supra*, 7.8.

37 Cf. *supra*, 9.3.3.

38 *Supra*, 9.9.

39 Cf. Whaley, *supra* note 9, p. 1399.

empower students to learn independently and to apply their general understanding and skills when they are faced with new legal issues.[40]

Third, there is always a next week or even the possibility to arrange for a make-up class if certain aspects cannot be addressed in one teaching session due to time constraints. Additional online teaching modules are another option to allow students to broaden their knowledge and deepen their understanding of certain aspects.

If it is necessary not to cover certain issues in class, one must of course ensure that the omission is properly communicated to students, who are normally grateful for reading suggestions on the respective topic. Obviously, examinations must of course be set in line (only) with what has been covered by the course.

10.12 Unprepared Teaching

I am stressing throughout this book that successful law teaching is a matter of proper preparation. Teachers should never go to class unprepared. And yet it can happen. I had explained in a previous section how I once thought that my co-teacher would teach the evening class while it was in fact my turn.[41] It worked out on that occasion because I had prepared my notes beforehand and was very familiar with the topic. But it can also happen, e.g. due to an emergency, that a teacher is thrown into a class on short notice, i.e. without time to prepare properly. The most basic decision to be made in such a scenario is whether to go ahead or to cancel the class and possibly arrange for a make-up class. As usual, there is no standard answer when cancellation is the proper choice, as the situation on the ground may vary significantly. However, there are some very simple issues to consider.

First, the cancellation may not be practical, and it may not even be possible to arrange for a make-up class. This could e.g. be the case very close to the term end or to the examination. One may also have to consider students' actual or potential reactions. Students may insist on in-class time not only because they have paid fees, but also because they have signed up for the complete in-class experience. Second, if the decision is made to go ahead with the class despite the lack of preparation, it would be inappropriate and easily spotted by students to fill in-class time with anything but proper content. Third, even without extensive preparation a law teacher might be able to fill a teaching session with Q&As related to the topic. I had mentioned earlier that it is helpful to have in place contingency arrangements in the form of exercises which can be used in order to fill available class time in a meaningful way.[42] However, it must of course be considered if this makes sense in light of the course contents to be covered and the pursued learning outcomes. The cancellation plus make-up class option can be the better way forward.

---

[40] *Ibid.*, p. 1400.

[41] *Supra*, 9.3.4.

[42] *Supra*, 9.10.

10.13 Grilling Law Students

I am emphasizing the importance which I place on interactivity in my classes in many chapters of this book.[43] I have also explained that I normally do not wait for students to raise their hands, but rather call upon students randomly to answer my questions. I had also mentioned that I do this even in very big classes.[44] I understand that my approach can put a lot of stress on students. At least it does so during the first sessions of my courses. I also know, however, that my approach is very effective as it fosters deep learning,[45] it enhances the general atmosphere in the classroom and last but not least it keeps students awake. And students like it despite the stress factor. In fact, while some students have sometimes mentioned in their teaching evaluations that I am a tough teacher, my teaching evaluations have never contained even one complaint about me "grilling" students.

To be successful with my interactive approach it is of course necessary to adhere to certain principles. Students whom I pick are guided to the correct answer and always end up with a "Very good! Well done!" I have never ever given any student a hard time in class for not being able to answer my questions. Students may be really indisposed, which can happen in particular with part-time students who take evening classes after a long day at work. Here, I do not insist, but may promise to get back to that student later for a second chance:

> "No problem if you cannot answer this question now. I will get back to you later with an even better question which I trust you will enjoy. This question will now go to your neighbor … who will hate you for the rest of the evening …".

When I was a student, very few of our professors would interact with students. One of those who did was much tougher on us than I am on my students and sometimes even yelled at us in the classroom. Due to eye problems this professor was not able to fixate anybody and rather went for students who were dressed extravagantly or colorfully. For us as students it was therefore important to show up in a very boring outfit. And this is exactly what I did one day only to have a girl in a bright red dress with even brighter white dots sit next to me right before the class started. As I had feared, the professor spotted the dots, but did of course not ask the girl to answer his question, but her neighbor, me. I had no clue how to answer his question and could just think about how terrible that red dress next to me looked. The professor seemed to think differently, the red dress must have calmed him down somehow as he did not even yell at me. I always tell my students this story when I explain why I am grilling them in class and that nobody has to be afraid. Everybody seems to see the logic in the red dress-story and even be happy with the grilling experience. I have added some personal flavor to my teaching, and I have communicated my teaching approach to my students. Mission accomplished!

---

[43] Cf. in particular *supra*, 9.4.

[44] *Ibid.*

[45] *Supra*, 7.8.

10.14 Unwelcome In-Class Surprises

Like any other teachers, law teachers must sometimes face unexpected situations in class which can be rather challenging. I once expected a phone call during class time from a lawyer I worked with on a cross-border investment project. In fact, I had intentionally indicated to that lawyer that I would be available during the teaching time, because I thought students would enjoy witnessing the real thing. The lawyer—whom I knew rather well—would also enjoy my announcement in class that he was now put on loudspeaker and that 100 students were listening and whether he had something to say to the next generation of lawyers. I normally turn off my phone before class, but this time I did not for those very reasons.

And then the phone really rang. I put on an important face, apologized, and informed students that I really had to take this call, which I thought was from an important client. When I answered the call it was no client, but my 84 years old aunt who had called to invite me to her 85th birthday. I adore my aunt and I felt very sorry that she could not handle the situation when I told her that I was standing in front of 100 students in the classroom who were listening to her. She just hung up on me. But my students loved it when I explained how I had wanted to show off with my lawyer client and we all had another good laugh.

On another occasion I had the terrible experience that I was unable to remember the name of the international convention I had been discussing for the past five minutes. I guess it was something like a blackout. Anyway, it was embarrassing, some students even started giggling while I was struggling to cope with the situation. What I should have done was to simply say it. I should have said that I had something like a blackout and that I would provide the information later—sorry! In fact, very often the best way forward in class is to just explain things as they are, maybe with a joke, and to carry on. Law students are mature enough to know that things happen.[46] They only cannot accept when the teacher tries to fool them.

The most common unwelcome surprise which almost every teacher must face from time to time are student questions to which the teacher does not have an answer. There is nothing wrong with such a situation—only newcomers get nervous. Law teachers are not walking encyclopedias and it is only normal that they do not know everything. Therefore, there is no need to pretend and this could even backfire when the answer turns out to be wrong later. In fact, the revelation that an answer is wrong can hit quickly if students smell something and do a quick online check. No good! It is therefore often much better to simply explain that the question sounds very interesting, that the teacher does not know the answer right away but will investigate the matter and revert to this issue next week. Of course, this should not happen too often. If it does, the approach in terms of proper preparations for each week's teaching session must be reconsidered.

[46]Whaley, p. 1396.

10.15 Difficult Students

10.15.1 General

Some time ago I heard a colleague saying that there are no difficult students, but only students a teacher has difficulties to cope with. This may be correct. Nevertheless, every law teacher knows that teaching can become really challenging when students are uncooperative. This section is not meant to provide a scientific analysis of action and reaction in situations of this kind. It rather explores possible reasons and ways to address situations of this kind that I have used in the past.

Two types of students can cause challenges in class, i.e. special needs students and uncooperative or otherwise challenging students. I will only very briefly talk about the former type but focus on the latter.

10.15.2 Special Needs Students

Special needs students are students with pathological physical or mental conditions. In particular mental conditions are often hard to detect and they are probably more common than law teachers are aware of as the following excerpt from a report on a US-based study indicates:

> "(B)y the spring of their 1L year, 32% of law students were clinically depressed, despite being no more depressed than the general public (about 8%) when they entered law school. By graduation, this number had risen to 40%. While this percentage dropped to 17% two years after graduation, the rate of depression was still double that of the general public."[47]

Great care is needed when working with special needs students, because law teachers are normally not trained to deal with cases of this kind and there is a risk that things go wrong.[48]

As a starting point, special needs students should be treated like any other students. However, special attention and more patience may be required. Teachers should also familiarize themselves with action to be taken in emergency situations, i.e. when professional help is needed. These situations may seem to be rather hypothetical, but they should have been thought through to know where and how support is available. In the interest of students' well-being the call for professional help should go out sooner rather than later.

---

[47] Cf. Clarke, p. 405.

[48] Cf. Tait, pp. 93–102.

10.15.3 Challenging Students

The other student type is challenging for the teacher for other than pathological reasons. I remember one day during my very early days as law teacher asking a student one of my usual in-class questions. This student's reaction was very aggressive: "I do not want to answer questions! I want to be left alone and just listen!"

This was my first experience of this kind and I had no idea what to do. So, after a brief moment I took a deep breath and said: "Okay, if this is the case, we will just take a different approach."

And then I explained that what would follow was very important for the examination. I continued with a high-speed monologue which barely allowed students to follow. I finished 15 min before the official class end time and left right away without further explanations. Prior to the following week's class three students were waiting for me outside the lecture theatre. They explained that that other student was a difficult character but did not really mean it. They begged me to get back to my original teaching style and to simply ignore that student. And so I did and everybody seemed happy. Even the student I had picked on the week before.

Some years later I had a student who was very good in answering my questions. He was polite, eloquent, and smart. But when it came to group work, he simply refused to talk to other students. He was just sitting on his place alone pretending to read without responding to others' attempts to include him. I am not sure why, but in this situation, I indicated to the other students to leave this one alone and I finished my course with—according to my humble opinion—great success. I think I had intuitively felt that it would not be possible to force group work upon that student. Since no marks were given for any in-class work I also did not see the point in making any efforts. His decision!

Another student a couple of years ago responded to my question addressed to her with: "Sorry, not tonight. I am really not in the mood." I left also this one alone. Her decision!

Sometimes opposition from students is caused by what could be called the "crack-authorities-game". Some students simply enjoy challenging the in-class leadership of the teacher. It normally takes some time to overcome related issues, but with a bit of patience it has always worked for me. There may not be a real problem, just some misunderstanding or a lack of ability on the student's or teacher's side to communicate properly in the classroom. I once had a mature student who challenged almost everything I introduced in class. When I organized a social event for this class outside the regular teaching time, I was surprised to see him happily joining and enjoying himself chitchatting away with others including myself. Maybe I had simply misjudged him.

The opposite type of challenging students are the weak students. In one of my very first years as a law teacher I was teaching a private law tutorial and a first-year student broke down in tears when she was not able to answer my question. I did not really pay attention to this student, but turned to the class and said something like this:

> Alright, I think I should talk a little bit about studying law. When I entered law school I did so as the No.1 student of my entire secondary school cohort. For the first two years in law school I never failed a test. However, I never got any grade better than average and most of the time I barely passed. This was extremely frustrating, because I had started my law studies with lots of self-confidence. It took me more than two years to understand how law works and what was required to succeed in my studies. I eventually graduated after five years, of which I had spent one in Shanghai studying modern Chinese history, i.e. something completely unrelated to law. I was not the No. 1 in my graduation cohort, but I did quite well.
>
> Thinking in law terms is just different from anything else and most students need some time to get going. Therefore, if you feel a bit lost now you are not different from me when I was at your stage. There is nothing to worry about for now. There is even less to worry about later changing your career path if you decide that law is not your thing. But, you should really give it a try, as law is the most interesting subject one can think of!

About fifteen years later, when I had already moved to Hong Kong, I received an email from that student who just wanted to say hello as she had come across my name online. She also wanted to thank me for what I had done for her during that tutorial. As she put it, I had addressed the issue in a rather factual way and given her all the re-assurance she needed. She later graduated successfully in law and was at the time of writing to me on partner-track with a magic circle firm.

Another form of challenge is caused by students who do not pay attention in class. For my own classes, this situation hardly ever happens, simply because everything is very interactive, and all students are engaged and engaging. Also, I must admit that if I spot a student who does not give me the attention which I feel I deserve, the next question is certainly hers or his, normally delivered with a broad smile and a remark like: "Mam/Sir, you do not seem to pay particular attention to my wonderful elaborations. This of course deserves immediate punishment. Therefore, the next question goes to you: …".

In-class situations can get out of control, and a law teacher needs to do everything to prevent this to happen. As trivial as it sounds, it is most important to remain professional and not to lose control. There are drastic examples of teachers responding to misbehaving students in class. I know about one case which even ended in court. Therefore, de-escalation must always be the main goal, even if this requires the teacher to hold back if this is at all possible and justifiable. The teacher must remember that she is performing a professional role which only aims at achieving the prescribed learning outcomes.

I will never forget a very embarrassing scene I once encountered on a flight from Hong Kong to Germany. My German neighbor had ordered some drinking water, and when the flight attendant brought a paper cup with water, he demanded a bottle—I suspect, because he had seen bottles being served in the business class. When the flight attendant explained that only paper cups of water were served in economy class, my neighbor freaked out and yelled at the flight attendant that this was outrageous and that he could pay for his bottle of water, pulling out some banknotes and throwing them via my face at the flight attendant. The flight attendant remained absolutely calm and replied: "Sir, throwing money at me is very impolite. I will get you your bottle of water in a moment. But we are on an airplane and you must remain calm, please." With this, she turned around and got the bottle of water for that man. I first did not understand how this behavior could be tolerated, but had to acknowledge that it worked. That nasty passenger calmed down for the rest of the flight whereas his seat neighbor was boiling with anger.

A law teacher does not need to serve bottled water. And yet, it may be necessary to de-escalate critical situations in the classroom. How this can be achieved depends on each case and can indeed be very challenging. It is key to understand what the reasons of the problems are. For example, if I am challenged by a young male student, who does not like to be told off by another, much older man in front of his peers, than this acknowledgement allows me to determine how to respond. I need to find a way to communicate with this student which does not conflict with his understanding of himself. Normally the mere act of giving (well-deserved!) attention can solve the problem. Having said that, law teachers must also ensure that students understand who is ultimately leading the class. The teacher needs to stay in control,[49] while at the same time treating students with professional respect.

A less drastic annoyance in the classroom appears to be a lack of attention on the students' part. As I had explained earlier, in recent years this has been exacerbated by the availability of all sorts of e-devices. I was even asked some years ago to do a presentation on this topic.[50] Core parts of my presentation went like this.

Nowadays in almost every meeting of lawyers everybody is using smartphones, laptops, or iPads to take notes, but also to check emails, to work on drafts or to check on stock prices. Even for conference panels it is not uncommon that speakers are checking their smart phones for messages while others are presenting. In fact, lawyers who are checking emails during events are showing how important they are. Why should students not be allowed to do the same?

From a more general point of view, again it simply cannot be assumed that students are not mature enough to decide what they should or should not do in the classroom. I had mentioned earlier[51] that when I went to law school, for the last two years prior to the final Legal State Examination I did not attend any lectures at all, because I did not consider lectures as an effective and efficient way of preparing for those exams. My decision! Students who attend lectures, even if they play with their electronic devices, are doing better than I did. Moreover, students who are using electronic devices in the classroom are multi-tasking. They try to follow the lecture and work on their devices at the same time. Is this not exactly what lawyers do and is this therefore not great training?

Nevertheless, many law schools have been through formal or informal discussions as to whether e-devices should be prohibited during teaching sessions. I heard about colleagues whose teaching evaluations dropped by two points when they introduced the prohibition to use smart phones in class. In my class I ask all students to put their phones away and I explain why this is important. Of course, some students still

[49] *Supra*, 7.6.

[50] Cf. Wolff 2014.

[51] *Supra*, 7.8.

use their smart phones from time to time, they just cannot help it. They get a kind reminder and—with a broad smile—the next question.

10.16 The "Why-Do-They-Cheat?" Problem

I have mentioned above[52] that I found skills training exercises particularly useful for substantive law teaching. Students explore underlying substantive law issues through active work on practical problems for the sake of sustainable acquisition of legal knowledge. This pedagogical rationale does, however, not always match students' thinking, as the case of my LIBT[53] course demonstrates.

During the third year of delivering the LIBT course I had to discover that students were not only using course materials (including lecture notes, question papers and model answers) handed out in previous years. Students even seemed to have complete write-ups of all my past LIBT teaching sessions. While it is common in Hong Kong for students to record lectures, I had not imagined that transcripts had been prepared and passed on to students of subsequent years. Many students had the materials on their laptops and consulted them during class time. Sometimes this led to almost comical situations. For example, when discussing legal aspects of the transport of export goods I always have to draw attention to the rather obvious fact that sea transport is of course impossible when goods are to be delivered to a landlocked country. In the past I normally employed the example of a consignee from Vientiane, the capital of Laos, and I normally started the discussion with the question where Vientiane is located. Having just returned from a conference in Austria in one year I changed the example and asked about Vienna. One student immediately volunteered to answer my question. She insisted that Vienna was the capital of Laos even after I had clarified that I had varied the question.

Apart from copyright issues potentially caused by students' reproduction and distribution of complete lectures without authorization, the availability and use of past materials creates obvious challenges from a pedagogical point of view. For example, during one LIBT skills training exercise one student reported on drafting errors in certain legal documents by simply reading out the model answer from her laptop computer. Furthermore, I must admit that it is not particularly amusing if students start laughing before I crack a joke in class, which—admittedly—I always do at the same point of a particular teaching session.[54]

It is difficult to understand what causes (mainly Asian) students to rely on past materials, given that performance in-class is not part of my LIBT assessment regime. I have not been able to obtain a definite answer from students. Different factors may

---

[52] *Supra*, 5.3.

[53] *Ibid.*

[54] Cf. *infra*, 10.17.1. about my own disappointment as a student when I had to discover that my professor was recycling his jokes; Prosser, p. 264, reporting on the same phenomenon as early as in 1948.

play a role. For example, students who are unfamiliar with interactive teaching or who feel insecure about their language skills may rely on past materials to boost their self-confidence. Other students seemed to regard the skills training exercises as part of a competition, in which it was their task to outsmart the teacher. Another explanation, offered by a colleague who is Asian herself, is that students simply want to prepare for classes in the best possible way.

After I first discovered the problem, I decided to tackle the matter proactively. I explained in class that the use of past materials was not in the best interest of anybody, as it spoils the intended learning experience, jeopardizes the chance to get training for exam questions and destroys the possibility to prepare for future work. Also, it takes away the fun of the exercises. Much to my surprise the only effect my appeal had, was that students tried to conceal related materials in class, or they had studied them intensively at home. Repeated explanations and appeals on my part did not seem to help much.

Contrary to the assumption that students should be mature enough to decide if and how they want to benefit from skills training exercises, I therefore announced as a preliminary measure that laptops and any hard copy materials could not be used during the in-class skills training exercises. Again, much to my surprise this was accepted without any objection. I also re-arranged the use of some skills training modules by moving them from one week to another to make it slightly more difficult to rely on previous year's materials or transcripts. These ad hoc measures were supplemented by the preparation of additional sets of skills training modules to be used in alternative years. The combined efforts seemed to solve the in-class problem to some extent, but left me wondering why I was forced to fool students for their own benefit.

In last year's LIBT class I arranged for a negotiation exercise and divided the class of 60 into small A-groups and B-groups of 3–5 members each. According to the question paper, each student group was to prepare a structuring proposal for their clients and then negotiate their output with representatives of the other side, i.e. each B-group with one A-group and vice versa. Shortly before the start of the negotiations I saw that one student had the lecture notes from the previous year with the key points of the exercise in front of her on the desk. This was even though I had announced that all materials should be stored under the table or in students' bags. Angry as I was, I announced that the group of this student was disqualified and quickly drew members from other groups to form one additional group to take the place of the disqualified one. While others were happily negotiating their results, the three members of the wrongdoer's group were sitting in the middle of the classroom, not knowing what to do. In fact, I could see that they were miserable not only because of the name-and-shame situation, but also because they missed the fun of the exercise. At one point one member of that group, a more mature part-timer, approached me and said that this was not fair, because her classmate had really not looked at the past lecture notes and anyway the other two group members were not guilty at all. At this point the wrongdoer student started crying bitterly and I felt terrible. I have learned my lesson and will not do this again! It was just too drastic. But for the rest of the term I did not detect any more cases of unauthorized use of materials. And I should also mention that I simply treated the wrongdoer student like any other student in the subsequent sessions. Everything went smoothly and even my teaching evaluations were not affected by this incident at all.

10.17 Teaching Gimmicks

10.17.1 General

Over time every teacher develops her own teaching tools which can be used to cheer-up the class, to redirect students' attention back to the taught subject or to otherwise enhance the learning environment.[55] I had reported about some of these tools in earlier sections. Below are some more.

Of course, teaching gimmicks need to be developed by each teacher individually. Remember that personal features (that regular little cough, the word "funky" that the teacher uses too often, the teacher's bowtie, the teacher's red sox or pink shirts etc.) can make it easier for students to remember the teacher, the teaching and—more importantly—to internalize the taught substance. At the same time, one must be careful not to overdo it. In particular, when it becomes clear that a joke is used repeatedly, students may get annoyed. For example, when I was a student, a friend who was one year ahead of me once reported during a coffee break about the great fun they had in class when one of the professors mimicked how heads of state meet as members of the European Council. The next year I had registered for the same course and that professor made the same funny remark at exactly the same point of his lecture. Being a law teacher now, I know that it is difficult to reinvent the wheel every year and that one would of course use again what had worked in the previous year. I therefore have admitted in the previous section that my teaching relies on tried and tested teaching tricks as well. But, back then as a student I was sincerely disappointed.

10.17.2 RTFQ

Often students do not answer the question they are being asked. Or they do not exactly answer the question. Whenever this happens the first time in my class, I explain to the student concerned that I am grateful that she has given me this particular answer because this also often happens in examinations, where it can be fatal:

> "Any deviation from what is asked can be a killer. It can be a killer in the exam, and it can also be a killer in your future professional life, e.g. because your client may not be happy about your comments on an issue she had not raised. Or, in court a judge may get very angry if you are not providing exactly the information requested. Therefore, remember:"

---

[55] Cf. Prosser, p. 264.

With this I turn around and write in big letters on the white board:

> "RTFQ!"

Then I turn to students again, I wait for a moment before I explain:

> "RTFQ! 'Read the Question!' This is the most important thing in an examination. Read the question, think about the question and answer the question! Answer only the question which is being asked! Nothing else! Make sure that you do understand which question is being asked! Remember that if you answer another question you may fail or your client may drop you."

Throughout a course I normally have several opportunities to issue RTFQ-reminders. And yes, the "F" makes its own contribution to the learning environment.

10.17.3 Calling Upon Students

When I was in my post-graduation state-run legal traineeship, we had one instructor who used the following sentence:

> "And this question will be answered by Frau Maier. … Don't look at me, Frau Maier is sitting over there."

Without turning around, he would point over his shoulder to the other side of the lecture venue where Frau Maier was indeed sitting. I have plagiarized this one and students love it. A variation is:

> "And this question will be answered by Ms Yip."

What follows is normally silence, and after a short moment I would continue:

> "… But, there is always a Ms Yip, so please identify yourself to the course teacher."

And her peers would be giggling and look or even point at poor Ms Yip who gets the question with a broad smile on my part.

Latecomers are also a lot of fun:

> "Apologies, I am late.",

says the very polite part-time student in his designer suit while he rushes to a free seat. My reply:

> "No problem. But being late must be punished. Before you get seated, here is the next question for you: …"
>
> Or:
>
> "Being late is of course a very serious matter. If this happens again, I will have to ask you to stand in the corner for the rest of the session."

A student who always sat in the first row once picked this line up immediately with a laugh:

> "… with your face towards the wall of course!"

10.18 When and Why Do Classes Go Wrong?

It is difficult to conclude based on the previous sections when and why classes go wrong. But they sometimes do. We all know that. Sometimes it is not even our fault. On other occasions we are just not focused, we did not prepare properly, or we are just not in a good mood. The bottom line is that this can always happen. If the teaching is otherwise fine, students will understand. But it should not happen too often!

Chapter 11
Examinations

11.1 General

A broad body of literature is available on the goals[1] and different forms as well as other aspects of law school examinations. It is not the purpose of this section to offer a literature review and to assess the different options. In line with the spirit of this book, this section elaborates briefly and in a rather non-scientific way on my own experience with some aspects of law school examinations. Furthermore, this section is only about summative assessments, while I hope that the interactive mode which I adopt in my classes provides my students with ample opportunity to receive summative feedback from me and their peers.

11.2 The Stress Factor Again

Some students take exams relatively easy, others struggle. But there is certainly always a degree of stress involved. It is for this reason that after I had qualified to practice in England and Wales, I swore to myself that I would never take an examination again. Then, seven years ago, I started a Cantonese course. Much to my surprise at the end of the first module there was a 30-min test. The test was optional and was in no way important for moving on to the next course level. But of course, I took the test. Maybe I just wanted to prove myself how easy and relaxed I nowadays am. 10 min into the test, I started sweating. After 20 min, the first classmates had finished and began leaving the venue. After 22 min, I felt my heart beating faster. After 25 min, I thought I had palpitations and was wondering whether continuing might entail health risk on my part. After 29 min, I had finished and submitted to the teacher my examination paper. After 30 min, I realized that my shirt was wet through

[1]Cf. for the difference between formative and summative assessments cf. e.g. Derell, https://www.aiuniv.edu/blog/2015/june/formative-vs-summative.

© The Author(s), under exclusive license to Springer Nature Singapore Pte Ltd. 2021
L.-C. Wolff, *The Art of Law Teaching*, SpringerBriefs in Law,
https://doi.org/10.1007/978-981-15-9148-8_11

and through. After one week I got my examination paper back—I had passed with the highest mark, a straight A.

I told my students about this experience during the next teaching session. As expected, they loved it. I had once again shared one of my stories. However, I told them that, while this experience has reminded me that exam situations can be stressful, I would not change the way I set and mark examinations. After all, the stress factor had pushed me to an A and that's what I wished for them. I had also once again communicated with my students about how I teach, this time about examinations.

It is important that examinations are also stressful for teachers, as they need to ensure that the examination hits the right level of difficulty, that the exam questions are clear, that announcements are made correctly and that students are properly prepared or else problems may be the consequence. Examinations are no-nonsense business for students and the same must hold true for teachers.

11.3 Setting Examinations

When it comes to setting examinations, my personal preference are in-class, closed-book examinations.[2] I have explained in an earlier section[3] why I prefer closed-book over open-book examinations. I prefer in-class examinations over take-home examinations simply because I trust that they are fairer. We never know who exactly is writing a take-home examination paper. COVID-19 has of course changed the teaching environment for all of us. In-class examinations are rare nowadays. And unexpectedly this has not led to many problems in my institution.

My exam papers normally comprise four questions out of which students must answer … four. This is for an examination time of three hours, which is standard in my faculty. I do not give students choices. Again, I trust that this is fairer, as no question is exactly like the other, and if all students must answer the same questions, they find a level playing field. They also do not waste time trying to find out which question is the easiest.

I nowadays do not use open-ended essay-type questions, as these are more difficult to mark fairly. More importantly, since my teaching sessions are problem-based—remember that I am using the FC approach and thus am filling all the in-class time with exercises[4]—three out of these four examination questions normally mirror the in-class exercise format. In fact, I often use examination questions of previous years, sometimes in a slightly modified way, for in-class exercise purposes.[5]

Out of the four examination questions, one question, which carries only 20 out of 100 marks, normally does not follow the pattern of in-class exercises. This question only asks several short questions. For example, a question may comprise ten terms or

---

[2] Cf. Sherry/Terrill/Laurens, pp. 1–26; Cahill-Ripley, pp. 206–218; Donnelly, pp. 105–109.

[3] *Supra*, 10.9.

[4] *Supra*, 9.3.3.

[5] Cf. *supra*, 9.4.

abbreviations from the taught topics which students must explain "in not more than three sentences each". Alternatively, students may be asked to explain the differences of ten pairs of terms or abbreviations "in not more than three sentences each". The purpose of this question always is to allow students to demonstrate what they have studied and therefore to get, without a major risk to miss the point of the question, close(r) to the passing mark.

My examinations are normally rather difficult and long.[6] Again, fairness is the most important reason for this approach. I have experimented with easier examination questions and found that the marking is much more difficult, as all students write the same. More importantly, easy examination papers do not allow the good students to show their brilliance. I wish to acknowledge expressly that I do consider the pursued learning outcomes[7] when setting exams. This means that, if all students deserve 100 out of 100 marks, then they will get them. Unfortunately, such a situation has never happened in any of my courses.

I explain the rationale of my examination pattern to students each year on several occasions. I remind them that they must prepare or else they may fail. I remind them that the question paper will be long, that there will be a lot to read and that proper time management is very important. Teacher-student communication![8] I have hardly ever had any complaints or even enquiries about my examinations.

11.4 Class Attendance and Class Participation

Many teachers award marks for class attendance or class participation and these marks count for the final grade. I have never adopted this method for the following reasons:

As explained above,[9] students deserve to be treated like what they are, i.e. adults, and I believe that we should consequently accept their decision to attend classes or not. Granting marks for class attendance simply means to use a stick rather than a carrot to entice attendance.

I have also mentioned earlier that I do not even wait for students to participate in my classes. Instead, I call upon them to answer my questions or to engage them in other ways during in-class exercises. I trust that giving out marks for in-class participation as such or even for the quality of in-class participation of students may be difficult again from the fairness point of view. Questions for students are never the same and the in-class environment including the situation of the teacher and the students is also always different. This leads to the very high risk that the assessment

---

[6]Cf., *supra*, 11.2.

[7]Cf., *supra*, 3.3.

[8]*Supra*, 10.9.

[9]*Supra*, 10.6.

of students' in-class participation becomes somewhat random. Again, these are my thoughts and empirical evidence may prove me wrong.

11.5 Marking

Marking is often regarded the most unpleasant part of the job as a law teacher. While it may not be all that much fun to read the same answers again and again, it is important to understand that the outcome of this exercise is extremely important not only for the students concerned but also as a quality control measure for law teachers.

According to my experience it is possible—with a very strict focus and depending on the examination as well as the length and clarity of students' writings—to mark about three to four examination papers per hour. Nonetheless, after having marked about twenty examination papers in one day, I normally need to stop and do something else, as concentration is fading and it would simply be unfair to continue. I have heard of colleagues who are able to get more papers done in a day, but for me this does not work.

Marking is facilitated if the model answer scheme provides for a clear breakdown of marks for different parts of the answer and other aspects such as structuring and clear language. It is important, however, that ultimately marking is a matter of academic judgment.

Chapter 12
Teaching Evaluations

Different jurisdictions and—within different jurisdictions—different institutions have varying arrangements regarding teaching evaluations ("TEs"). Some law schools do not have TEs at all, some do TEs only for some courses, others have TEs across all courses.

Differences also exist in relation to the way how TEs are conducted. Normally they are based on student feedback. In the past, they were often paper-based and e.g. conducted during one of the last teaching sessions of a course by third parties with the teacher leaving the room. Nowadays online TEs are gaining popularity, often at the price of a significant drop in terms of the response rate. Normally TEs comprise questionnaires which generate a general score for the teacher benchmarked against school or programme mean score or any other mean score such as the one at undergraduate or postgraduate level. Sometimes results are "normalized", with extreme scores not being counted. Sometimes TEs are conducted more than once per term, as in my university, where at undergraduate level an early feedback system has been installed to allow students to make themselves heard within the first six weeks of a course.

Student TEs should first be conducted for formative reasons, i.e. they should aim to allow teachers to engage in an informed self-reflection with the ultimate goal to improve their teaching. In practice, TEs seem to be seen mainly as a tool for staff assessment. TEs face lots of criticism, and it is not surprising that such criticism comes mainly from those teachers whose TEs are not the best. The main arguments are as follows:[1]

Low response rates in TE exercises mean that they are not completely reliable. Furthermore, TEs conducted by students have only limited value for the question if learning outcomes have been achieved. At the most, they can offer an indication if the teaching and learning environment was or was not liked by students. Tough teachers will therefore receive less favorable evaluations. In particular, students who have been criticized by a teacher will naturally use the TEs to retaliate, and they

[1] Also cf. Claessens, pp. 43–54.

© The Author(s), under exclusive license to Springer Nature Singapore Pte Ltd. 2021

L.-C. Wolff, *The Art of Law Teaching*, SpringerBriefs in Law,
https://doi.org/10.1007/978-981-15-9148-8_12

know about their power. Finally, TEs are not reliable, because good students could not be bothered to participate, while it is rather the underperforming students who will use TEs to vent their frustrations.

All these are valid concerns, but it is a different question if the underlying assumptions are correct. According to my experience and other anecdotal evidence, TEs conducted by students are by and large reliable. They offer a rather accurate and objective picture of the teaching as well as the course as such. Low response rates do of course prohibit the assumption of statistical accuracy. But TEs may still carry indicative value. Furthermore, as far as I understand, it is rather the good students who participate in TEs, whereas other students stay away. I have mentioned in an earlier section that the assumption that tough teachers never do well in TEs may not be correct.[2] Finally, it is again important that also TEs ultimately relate to the very different question what good teaching really means and how success in teaching can be measured.[3]

Should we care about TEs? TEs can be rather painful when taken seriously by teachers. I had one colleague who refused to look at them because he did not want to allow students to upset him "for nothing", as he put it.

Normally a teacher knows how the course went and the TEs then confirm this feeling. Sometimes teachers are, however, not aware that their performance is not up to the required standard and TEs serve as an important reminder that one's own perception may not be in line with reality. But apart from the overall scores, TEs provide very good insights on aspects of the teaching or the course and how improvement can be achieved. It is this aspect which makes TEs indeed valuable and they should therefore be taken seriously.

There are also other forms of TEs, e.g. those done by colleagues, the Dean or Associate Dean(s) or externals who sit in classes and review the performance of the teacher. In my experience this and other non-student TE formats are not very common. Furthermore, the effectiveness of these exercises may be questionable mainly for two obvious reasons. First, one-off reviews may not be representative. Second, if informed upfront of the review, the teacher will certainly prepare for and deliver a tailored teaching session. If in contrast not informed upfront that a TE is to take place, the teacher may not even arrange for anything that is reviewable, e.g. in sessions where students do presentations.

---

[2] *Supra*, 7.6.

[3] Cf. *supra*, 7.2.

Chapter 13
Designing New Courses, Programmes, Law School Curricula

13.1 General

As a founding member of my own Faculty I was closely involved in the design of six undergraduate and postgraduate law programmes and numerous courses. Moreover, during my five years as Dean of my university's Graduate School I had to work on many programme proposals across Faculties. In a way this has been very good training. I now know which language should be used, which boxes need to be ticked, which structures must be adopted and what will potentially cause problems during the approval process. I trust that I could write course and programme proposals in many areas about which I do know absolutely nothing. Having said that, before a teacher or an institution begins to work on the creation of particular courses or programmes, the goals to be pursued, the substantive knowledge and the skills to be instilled and in many instances also the teaching methods to be applied should be very clear to all concerned parties.

In most institutions the creation of new courses and programmes must follow a certain administrative process. While this is often regarded as unnecessary red tape, it must be remembered that quality control must play a major role in any educational and research enterprise and procedural rules normally aim at ensuring just this.

13.2 Why Setting up New Programmes and Courses?

In a perfect world programmes and courses are designed for pedagogical reasons, i.e. because they are useful for students, for the institution and the society at large. Whether in line with this rationale or not, one can observe that new programmes and courses focus on areas and themes which are somewhat fashionable in certain periods of time. For example, in the 1970s international law became very trendy. In the 1980s the focus may have been on human rights and criminal justice. The 1990s and the early years of the new millennium probably saw a concentration on corporate

© The Author(s), under exclusive license to Springer Nature Singapore Pte Ltd. 2021
L.-C. Wolff, *The Art of Law Teaching*, SpringerBriefs in Law,
https://doi.org/10.1007/978-981-15-9148-8_13

governance and later corporate social responsibility. Nowadays law & technology is regarded as a sexy topic.

Realistically speaking, programmes and courses are not always established just for pedagogical reasons. For example, one can often hear that Master of Laws (LLM) programmes are often created as income generating vehicles ("cash cows") in the first place. In times when governments reduce the funding of educational and research enterprises almost everywhere this is not surprising. As long as there is a sufficient student demand and as long as the quality of the delivery is not compromised, financial motives do not have to lead to raised eyebrows, unless one supports the idea that education should be completely free of charge. The travel restrictions imposed because of the COVID-19 pandemic have made it impossible for students to study abroad. Many law schools in the USA, Australia and the UK that have relied on related fee income are now facing severe difficulties.[1]

Another problem is that quality programmes are in most cases resource intensive and institutions must consider carefully if they can cope. I have seen programmes where over 90% of the courses were taught by external part-time teachers. Reasons for such an arrangement could e.g. be that part-time teachers have special expertise which is not available in-house or that external teachers are simply cheaper because only the hourly rates, but no overhead needs to be factored in. Programmes which are delivered by external teachers do not at all have to be deficient in terms of quality. However, programme ownership may be an issue when the institutional role is reduced to programme management rather than programme delivery.

13.3 Joint and Dual Degree Programmes

In recent years joint and dual degree programmes have become very popular across the globe. In fact, I have always dreamed of a law programme where students study law in at least three different jurisdictions. The goal of such an inter-jurisdictional education would not be to award to the students three instead of just one degree, but to broaden students' legal and personal horizons.[2] Acknowledging the benefits of internationally trained lawyers, I trust that institutions should do everything to facilitate study abroad options of any kind. I would go even further and suggest that students should be required to study abroad for a certain time for their own professional and personal benefit.

Study abroad options can be set up through co-operations between providers of legal education located in various jurisdictions different forms are available, such as student exchanges, joint or dual degree programmes, which may or may not combine undergraduate and postgraduate study options. Feasibility depends on institutional strategies, resources, and administrative settings.

[1] Sloan, https://www.law.com/2020/04/23/law-schools-hit-by-financial-fallout-from-covid-19/?slreturn=20200901034142.

[2] Cf. Bosch, pp. 284–296.

Over the last decade dual degree programmes which are operated based on the two-for-one principle have become rather popular. Here, students study at two different institutions. Through credit transfer arrangements or other mechanisms both institutions recognize credits earned by the student at the respective other institution and eventually the student can obtain two degrees while de facto having fulfilled graduation requirements for only one. The academic viability of arrangements of this kind may be questionable, although it must be acknowledged that studying in different environments, with different foci and at different levels deserve to be considered. As a rule of thumb two degrees should require at least fulfilment of 150% of the graduation requirements of both degrees.

Chapter 14
The Teacher-Student Relationship

Many sections of this book discuss different aspects of teacher-student relationships. This section elaborates further on this important topic based on my own experience. In fact, I have seen it (almost) all. I have had and am still receiving very nice thank-you emails from current and former students on a regular basis. However, there are also other cases.

Many years ago, when marking exam papers of an in-class closed-book exam of my course, I found a Tang Dynasty love poem in one of the scripts, whatever that meant. I had one student who would lead friends and family to the front window of my office, so that they could look at me while explanations where given which I was (fortunately) not able to hear from inside. Another student sent me expensive gifts, which I had to return through the Faculty. One student wrote to me informing me that he would come to Hong Kong on a certain date and when I asked a colleague who was familiar with the background of that student's case, what to do, I was advised "just to be careful". I am also aware of teacher-student interactions which ended up in court and I know about encounters which are too embarrassing and sensitive to be told here.

I wish to emphasize that all of these are special cases and they did happen at various universities at different times. But, for teachers and for students every one of those can be quite nerve-wracking. And one does not necessarily see them coming. As for me, I am not aware of anything that could have triggered any abnormal reaction, although I had mentioned earlier[1] that I have changed my teaching style since coming to Asia by adopting a less engaging approach due to the different cultural environment. Before discussing if and how "extreme situations" can be avoided or dealt with, it is necessary to reconsider the special features of the teacher-student relationship.

Teacher-student relationships are human-to-human relationships and one may argue that the situation in law schools is not different from interactions between human beings in any other setting. While this is of course correct, there are special aspects which must not be forgotten.

---

[1] *Supra*, 9.5.

© The Author(s), under exclusive license to Springer Nature Singapore Pte Ltd. 2021

L.-C. Wolff, *The Art of Law Teaching*, SpringerBriefs in Law,
https://doi.org/10.1007/978-981-15-9148-8_14

Law teachers, like other university teachers, are (perceived and actual) authorities because they lead the teaching and thus students' learning process. As such, law teachers are exposed. They are in the center of students' attention. I remember when I was a student, we had sketches of some of our law professors drawn on the walls of the apartment that we shared amongst seven students. Whether in a good way or a bad way, they were special for us. We were gossiping about them. We observed how they behaved in class, how they responded to disruptions and what they were wearing. Any information about their private lives that we could get hold of was shared. Social media have made this kind of information sharing even easier.

As explained above,[2] when I was doing my second Ph.D., I was teaching tutorials while at the same time working for my supervisor. Students knew me. When I entered one of the student pubs in my small university town, 50% of the guests would turn their heads towards me and then discuss my arrival. The bitter reality from my point of view was that my university town had hardly anything other than student bars and that I could never have more than two beers or else rumors might spread the next day. My point is that law teachers simply must acknowledge that students care about them and their lives. In a way we are public figures, which again reinforces our authority.

And there is another aspect:

The law teacher position is a position of power. It is the teacher who eventually assesses the student and is therefore very important for students' future careers. From this point of view, the teacher-student relationship is one of dependence. I have mentioned throughout this book[3] that law students are adults and that we should treat them like adults. However, it is also important to acknowledge that law teacher and students are not on a par with each other and this can easily lead to challenges.

One does not need to be a psychologist to understand that because of all the above it is easy for students to become emotionally involved with their professors one way or another and that this can even take rather dramatic turns. It is crucial to acknowledge that this can happen so as to be able to take precautionary steps and to respond.[4]

The teacher-student relationship can of course not only become special for students. Numerous books and movies have described situations where a teacher becomes obsessed with a student or with students and the resulting difficulties. In fact, students also have powerful tools. Apart from the fact that they can play their juvenile charms, think about a young law teacher who cannot get her class under control, who gets complaints from students and who is slammed in her teaching evaluations. Or think about my own situation, as reported in an earlier chapter,[5] when I attempted a teaching demonstration as part of a recruitment process and the class just did not cooperate. Careers can be destroyed by students.

---

[2] *Supra*, 10.1.

[3] E.g. *supra*, 7.8.

[4] Also cf. *supra*, 10.16.

[5] *Supra*, 10.9.3.

The question is if and how these challenges can be avoided or how the risk of things getting out of control can at least be minimized. Furthermore, it must be considered what steps are available when real problems emerge because necessary pre-emptive measures have not been taken or have failed. Many cases are not just black and white and problem cases may not be easily detectable or they only become problematic over time. Furthermore, there may be pathological cases which require professional help[6] and teachers need to be prepared to make referrals sooner rather than later.

In different parts of the world views as to how much pastoral care universities should offer to their students may vary significantly. My personal view is that law teachers are ultimately (only) tasked to teach law and they should do this at the highest professional level. Law teachers can of course also be a point of contact for students in relation to issues which are not related to their studies. However, law teachers are not trained to deal with pathological situations and—as already said—if students show signs of these, they must be referred to units that are able to offer professional help.[7]

Leaving pathological cases aside, to avoid challenges arising out of the teacher-student relationship it is first crucial to maintain a professional distance. Law teachers cannot replace parents or friends of their students. It is not their job to solve emotional or even medical problems, but rather support their students to obtain professional help when needed. Needless to say, that law teachers should under no circumstances exploit their position as teachers. Absolute professionalism based on objectivity and impartiality are mandatory. This also means that emotions should not play any role on the teachers' part. Communications with students, whether face-to-face, over the phone, in letter form, by email or via learning platforms, via social media or in any other form must always be professional in terms of form and substance. Furthermore, law teachers are representing their institution. Internal matters—annoying as they may be—must not be shared with students, even if it is sometimes tempting to proclaim that all the bad things in the world are a result of the school's management. Anything else would be unprofessional.

As a matter of principle, I do never accept presents from my students, even when they are of minor value or just of symbolic nature. In Asia, where I am teaching now, this sometimes requires extensive explanations and apologies in order not to offend students who potentially only tried to do what appears rather normal in this part of the world. However, the strict application of my approach allows straight forward solutions in all cases and is in my view therefore preferable.

For all the reasons mentioned above, romantic or sexual relationships between teachers and students are extremely sensitive topics. They are often expressly prohibited in educational institutions e.g. through enacted Codes of Conduct. In interactions with students, teachers must take extra care to avoid even the slightest hint of impropriety and leave no room for misinterpretation. If anything beyond the professional interaction ever happens, an immediate disclosure to the teacher's supervisor(s) is

[6] *Supra*, 10.16.

[7] Ibid.

required and action must be taken to avoid any possibility of the student concerned, other students, the teacher, the institution or any other party being affected. What this exactly means must again be decided on a case by case basis. Sometimes measures of a rather drastic nature may be necessary.

Chapter 15
The Teacher-Teacher Relationship

Law teachers do not work in isolation, but with other faculty. In an ideal world the relationship amongst law teachers is harmonious, supportive, and collegial with everybody just working together for the same goal, i.e. good teaching, and research for the benefit of students, the institution, and the society as a whole. Reality does unfortunately not always correspond with this ideal. Like other work environments law schools have their own politics, probably exacerbated by the fact that success and contributions in academia can often not be assessed based on hard numbers. The teacher-teacher relationship is only indirectly relevant for law teaching. However, I still want to share briefly some of my stories and observations, because they were important for my professional life.

Many years ago, I had created and was teaching a particular course quite successfully, when a colleague submitted a proposal for a very similar course, with a slightly amended title, to the relevant committees in charge of approval. No need to mention that I had not been consulted. I was rather junior at that time and I had invested heavily in my course to make it work. I was stunned not primarily because I feared any impact on my course, but rather because of the viciousness that I had not expected. It took some discussion until it was decided that the new course proposal would not go forward due to the obvious overlaps.

The "stealing" of courses is not only such an effective tool to cause trouble because the creation of a new course and the preparation for classes requires a lot of work. Moreover, teaching normally gets much better after a teacher has taught a course two or three times.[1] Forcing a teacher to give up one and to take over another new course will therefore not only lead to additional work, but may also affect teaching evaluations. I have heard of law teachers who have considered not to go on sabbatical leave for fear that somebody else might grab their courses.

There are many other ways how colleagues may try to make each other's lives miserable. Examples are excessive scrutiny of examination papers in examination review panels, blocking of proposals e.g. regarding necessary curriculum changes or

[1] Cf. *supra*, 7.7.

© The Author(s), under exclusive license to Springer Nature Singapore Pte Ltd. 2021

L.-C. Wolff, *The Art of Law Teaching*, SpringerBriefs in Law,
https://doi.org/10.1007/978-981-15-9148-8_15

the addition of new electives, bad-mouthing of colleagues in class or in discussions with other colleagues or simply bullying. On one occasion the innocent and puzzled early-career me heard a colleague saying about another colleague that now "the pressure needed to be increased". It took me some time to understand what that meant. It is obvious that the atmosphere can be seriously poisoned when these things happen.

This is not the place to discuss how to deal with law school politics from the management point of view. However, self-confident leadership based on transparency, reliability and absolute impartiality is mandatory to avoid problems and to address related challenges. And it is important to communicate these core values again and again to the faculty.

From the perspective of individual law teachers, it must be acknowledged that politics can hardly ever be avoided entirely. Some teachers try. In one of my former universities one colleague kept hiding in his office, he never spoke up in meetings and in fact it seemed that everybody had forgotten about him. This was until he was heard while walking the law school corridors and excitedly yelling into his mobile phone: "Buy for one million, buy for one million …". He was the talk of the day again.

When politics kick in, one must be prepared that amicable solutions may not be achievable. Whether it is necessary in situations of this kind to involve others, in particular the management, depends on the specifics of the case. In my experience, as long as views are presented in a professional, i.e. unemotional and matter-of-fact manner based on sound arguments, they will be heard. Furthermore, if a teacher discharges her teaching, research and administrative duties successfully, there should be nothing to fear. However, as an old friend of mine used to say, "Sometimes you lose and sometimes you win. You just need to be prepared."

Chapter 16
Teaching Administration

Law teaching delivered at law schools or other teaching institutions requires a certain amount of administration. The law teacher is tasked to manage her own course. But normally school and university administration are involved as well. Systems differ significantly regarding the distribution of administrative duties to different levels and individuals. In some jurisdictions professors with their assistants and secretaries carry out most of the course and programme management. Elsewhere departmental units, the law school or sometimes central university units oversee different administrative tasks such as the allocation of teaching and examination times and venues. The existing variety is a result of different traditions and cultures, funding models and preferences.

Law teachers are regularly complaining about bureaucracy and unnecessary red tape. While this is often done with good reasons, teaching without any administration is also not possible. And, good administration can make a positive difference, while bad administration will lead to a lot frustration. The administrative part of law teaching can therefore not be ignored, even if this may be perceived as rather painful.

Administrative diligence on the part of the law teacher as well as the administrative staff is crucial to avoid hick-ups and annoyances. Sometimes special help from administrative colleagues is required e.g. to deal with emergency situations or to accommodate particular arrangements or simply to remedy the teacher's own omissions or errors, which do in fact happen occasionally even in law schools.

Administrative support can be required with routine tasks and on an ad hoc basis. The probably most common situation when ad hoc support is needed is the cancellation of a class, e.g. due to unavailability of the teacher. Examples are family emergencies or conference attendances during term time. In these scenarios make up classes must be arranged, and students need to be informed accordingly. A good and professional relationship with administrative colleagues will ensure that the required support is granted expeditiously.

Finally, every law teacher will at certain points of their careers have to serve in administrative positions such as those of course leaders, programme directors, department heads, associate deans or deans. One would assume that everybody chips

© The Author(s), under exclusive license to Springer Nature Singapore Pte Ltd. 2021
L.-C. Wolff, *The Art of Law Teaching*, SpringerBriefs in Law,
https://doi.org/10.1007/978-981-15-9148-8_16

in from time to time and that the required administrative work is therefore distributed evenly. In practice this is unfortunately not the case for a variety of different reasons. Last but not least, not every law teacher is an administration genius and not every law teacher enjoys administrative work.

Are administrative positions important from a career perspective? They certainly should be! In fact teaching, research and service are normally the three domains which are considered in staff appraisal and advancement exercises conducted in tertiary institutions. Different weightings may be given to contributions in the three domains with service (including internal and external administration) normally being the least important one. Nevertheless, advancement through the ranks always requires evidence of leadership, and strong administrative performance can be a big plus in this regard.

Chapter 17
Law Teaching in Times of Crises

Law schools and law teachers can be hit by very different types of crises:

- Health and safety crises like the COVID-19 pandemic;
- Social unrest;
- Crises in terms of student numbers and student quality as many U.S., UK and Australian law schools have experienced in 2020, when numbers of foreign fee-paying students declined as a result of COVID-19[1];
- Political crises which can manifest themselves in very different ways, including on-campus student protests;
- Institutional crises, e.g. because of power struggles at different levels;
- Technological crises, e.g. when the IT system is hacked or breaks down, inadvertent data leaks or when untested technology is introduced on short notice;
- Crises caused by staff movements and e.g. a resulting lack of teachers;
- Reputational crises, e.g. because of fake news about a teacher or the institution; and
- Personal crises of individual teachers.

All these crises might affect the work of law teachers and the operation of law schools in different forms. The question is if standard responses are available or if different crises must always be addressed in tailor-made manners.

It is certainly true that a one-size fits all approach cannot not work. However, it has also been correctly remarked that.

> crisis situations tend to share common elements. All are typically unexpected or develop in a manner that may take leaders by surprise; all require critical decision-making and communications with key stakeholders under intense time pressure; and all present the possibility of grave consequences if not managed effectively.[2]

---

[1]Cf. Sloan.

[2]Galvis/Giuffra Jr/Ahlers, https://latinlawyer.com/chapter/1177356/introduction-effective-crisis-management-in-latin-america.

© The Author(s), under exclusive license to Springer Nature Singapore Pte Ltd. 2021
L.-C. Wolff, *The Art of Law Teaching*, SpringerBriefs in Law,
https://doi.org/10.1007/978-981-15-9148-8_17

Correct decisions during crises can only be made based on comprehensive knowledge of the background and the current situation. Such knowledge is required at the level of law teachers, who need to deal with issues on the ground, and at the level of the institution for overall management purposes. It is key to identify actual and potential problems, to decide how to respond, to implement measures and to monitor and manage outcomes. In this regard, constant and open exchange of information between all concerned parties is crucial. For law teachers this may imply the need for an increased interaction with the institutional management, with other teachers, with students and with external parties. Time pressure is one of the special features of crises, for which reason law teachers may have to act and lead responses more pro-actively than in non-crisis times.

While the information flow is important, it must be managed.[3] To avoid misunderstandings, rumors or even fake news, information must only be disseminated once it is confirmed. This may require law teachers and their institution to stand firm even when pressure from students and other parties builds up because of the (understandable) desire to receive status updates. Careful and patient sharing of the reasons why information cannot yet be shared are key to keep developments under control.

Steps to be taken must align with institutional priorities and with the priorities of teachers. And these priorities must be defined and shared across different levels. For example, in times of COVID-19 these priorities should have been (i) health and safety of students, teachers and other staff, and (ii) students' educational interests as well as their professional advancement.

It is important that, if at all possible, normal law school life should go on despite a crisis. As already indicated, this requires all concerned parties, including law teachers, to adopt rather flexible approaches to be able to take quick and appropriate steps. Furthermore, crisis scenarios normally lead to additional work. COVID-19 is again a good example in this regard. Many law teachers did not only have to acquire online teaching skills in a short period of time, but also had to set additional exam papers e.g. for students who were unable sit regular online exams due to internet problems. Finally, law teachers have to deal with increased communication needs to overcome the effects of a crisis.

Every crisis also carries opportunities. During COVID-19 the whole law teaching world was able to build up significant online teaching capabilities. This may in turn have triggered considerations regarding alternative pedagogical approaches. It should also not be underestimated that crises can have very positive learning effects on the students' side. Like law teachers, also law students must respond to crises, they must deal with unexpected situations, they need to get organized and they may even have to deal with physical and psychological impact. All this triggers learning processes which law teachers can and should try to support. Are there nicer ways of teaching and learning? Of course! But this does not change the fact that crises always also teach lessons.

---

[3]Cf. Narayandas/Hebbar/Li, https://hbr.org/2020/06/lessons-from-chinese-companies-response-to-covid-19.

Chapter 18
Game Over for Law Teaching?

Richard Susskind has predicted that law, legal markets and thus the work of lawyers will see massive changes in the years to come.[1]

> Just as other professions are undergoing massive upheaval, then the same must now happen in law. Indeed, it is already happening. The bespoke specialist who handcrafts solutions for clients will be challenged by new working methods, characterized by lower labor costs, mass customization, recyclable legal knowledge, pervasive use of advanced technology, and more.[2]

Susskind argues that these changes are driven by three main factors. First, clients—including in-house lawyers—will require more and better services for the same or even less money.[3] Second, the ongoing liberalization of legal markets will create additional competition for the providers of legal services.[4] Third, the increasing use of legal technologies and in particular the rise of artificial intelligence (AI)[5] is already changing the legal world at a rapid pace. In fact, while the rise of AI will provide opportunities in the future which can hardly be imagined today,[6] AI is also taking away work from lawyers and is thus replacing them. Take due diligence as an example. Until only ten years ago, law firms could throw armies of young lawyers into the due diligence exercises and charge large amounts of money for their work.[7] Nowadays such tasks are largely discharged by AI. Along with all this comes the ongoing globalization of the world's economies, which makes it possible to outsource standard legal services to foreign jurisdictions where they are simply cheaper.[8]

---

[1] Cf. in general Susskind 2017.

[2] *Ibid.*, p. xix.

[3] *Ibid.*, pp. 4–5.

[4] *Ibid.*, pp. 5–10.

[5] Wolff 2020, p. 485.

[6] Ibid.

[7] Susskind 2017, pp. 10–15.

[8] *Ibid.*, pp. 36–42.

© The Author(s), under exclusive license to Springer Nature Singapore Pte Ltd. 2021

L.-C. Wolff, *The Art of Law Teaching*, SpringerBriefs in Law,
https://doi.org/10.1007/978-981-15-9148-8_18

As a result of all these developments, law and legal markets are indeed changing rapidly and legal education has to change as well.[9] New topics such as "legal entrepreneurship",[10] "legal project management",[11] "legal ops"[12] and last but not least "legal technologies"[13] will have to be covered. Legal education itself requires an increasing use of technologies to cater to the digital student generation, but also to become more cost-effective and to improve in terms of quality.[14] Needless to say that all this will affect the way how law teaching will be delivered, and it will therefore be of utmost importance for every individual law teacher.[15]

There are of course different types of technology which will play important roles in legal education over time. However, certainly the biggest changes will be seen when AI is on a broad scale introduced to legal education.

The notion of AI is not understood in the same, standardized way around the globe.[16] Generally speaking "AI" relates to machines and machine systems, normally computers and computer systems, which mirror human intelligence,[17] in particular the human learning process.[18] AI increases its capabilities like humans, who from their early childhood develop knowledge and skills over their life-time to very advanced levels as the following story shows.

> This is the story of AlphaGo Zero, the first artificial intelligence to learn *tabula rasa* – meaning from a 'clean slate' without any human input. AlphaGo Zero started out with no prior knowledge of the game Go except for its rules. Nonetheless, after forty days of playing against itself, it outperformed the algorithm that defeated the world's best human Go player.[19]

Anything new generates more learning activities until AI understands the new features and can use and advance it independently.[20] Once AI is able to mimic human behavior, then AI should obviously also be able to mimic law teachers and their teaching. In a perfect AI world, law classes may therefore no longer be conducted by human beings. Instead, they will be conducted by machines.

Does this sound scary? It does! Will we all use our jobs? Probably not immediately, but the future is uncertain. In fact, it is commonly understood that AI

---

[9] *Ibid.*, pp. 158–166; also cf. Tamanaha.

[10] *Supra*, 5.2.

[11] Cf. Miller, https://sterlingmiller2014.wordpress.com/2017/07/31/ten-things-legal-project-management-for-beginners/.

[12] Cf. Corporate Legal Operations Consortium, https://cloc.org/what-is-legal-operations/.

[13] Cf. *supra*, 5.2.

[14] Cf. Smith, pp. 209–221.

[15] See, however, *ibid.*, p. 185.

[16] The following is based on and partly borrowed from Wolff 2020, pp. 487–489.

[17] Wolff *ibid*.

[18] Christine N., https://www.iso.cuhk.edu.hk/images/publication/newsletter/536/html5/4/#zoom=z.

[19] Palace, pp. 218–219; cf. Denicola, pp. 251–287 (253).

[20] Wolff 2020, p. 488.

> will increasingly replace repetitive jobs. Not just blue-collar work, but a lot of white-collar work ... 40% of jobs in the world, including truck drivers', telesales people's, security guards' and even radiologists' will become displaceable by technology over the next 15 years.'.[21]

The development of a perfect AI world will take time. However, some AI experts have predicted that this is going to happen within the next 20 to 50 years.[22] "Combined results from surveys of artificial intelligence experts estimate a 50% chance of human-level machine intelligence by 2040 and a 90% probability by 2075".[23]

By that time, I will unfortunately no longer be involved. However, those who are currently starting their law teaching careers will have to consider the consequences with a very open mind.[24]

---

[21] Lee Kai-fu, former Apple, Microsoft and Google executive and now chairman of Sinovation Ventures, quoted by Christine N.; Palace, pp. 240–241; Denicola, pp. 255–256; also cf. Susskind, p. 12.

[22] Cf. Storrs Hall, p. 250.

[23] Denicola, *ibid.*, p. 256.

[24] Susskind, p. 13.

References

Note: All online references were last checked in October 2020.

Articles/Theses/Papers

Alexandra A, Seumas M (1999) Copyright in Teaching Materials. Educ Philos Theor 31:87–96

Batty R (2013) Well there's your problem—the case for using PBL to teach law to business students. Law Teacher 47:243–260

Bennet SC (2014) Distance Learning in Law. Seton Hall Legislative J 38:1–15

Biggs L, Hunter K (2014) Rethinking legal skills education in an LLB curriculum. J Juridical Sci 39(1):1–30

Blaze DA (2019) Law student motivation, satisfaction and well-being: the value of a leadership and professional development curriculum. Santa Clara Law Rev 58:547–566

Bobot L (2009) Teaching negotiation at the faculty of law of the sorbonne university. Eur J Legal Educ 5:13–22

Bosch GS (2009) The "internationalization" of law degrees and enhancement of graduate employability: European dual qualification degrees in law. Law Teacher 43:284–296

Cahill Ripley A (2015) Innovative methods of assessment in law: the value of open-book exams as a catalyst for improving teaching and learning in the law school. Law Teacher 49:206–218

Caplow S, Fullerton M (2005) Co-teaching international criminal law: new strategies to meet the challenges of a new course. Brooklyn J Int Law 31:103–127

Case SM, Donahue BE (2008) Developing high-quality multiple-choice questions for assessment in legal education. J Legal Educ 58:372–387

Claessens SJFJ (2020) The role of student evaluations in a PBL centred law curriculum: towards a more holistic assessment of teaching quality. Law Teacher 54:43–54

Clarke BS (2014–15) Coming out in the classroom: law professors, law students and depression. J Legal Educ 64:403–415

Clarke S, Blissenden M (2013) Assessing student group work: is there a right way to do it? Law Teacher 47:368–381

Clough J, Shorter GW (2015) Evaluating the effectiveness of problem-based learning as a method of engaging year one law students. Law Teacher 49:277–302

Combe MM (2014) Selling intra-curricular clinical legal education. Law Teacher 48:281–295

Coper M (2012) My top ten tips for good deaning. J Legal Educ 62:70–80

Denicola RC (2016) Ex machina: copyright protection for computer generated works. Rutgers Univ Law Rev 69:251–287

© The Author(s), under exclusive license to Springer Nature Singapore Pte Ltd. 2021
L.-C. Wolff, *The Art of Law Teaching*, SpringerBriefs in Law,
https://doi.org/10.1007/978-981-15-9148-8

Donnelly L (2002) A modest proposal: the case for the open-book law exams. Eur J Legal Educ 2:105–109
Draper MJ, Gibbon SG, Thomas J (2018) Lecture recording: a new norm. Law Teacher 52:316–334
Dziuban C, Graham CR, Moskal PD, Norberg A, Sicilia N (2018) Blended learning: the new normal and emerging technologies. J Educ Technol Higher Educ 15 https://doi.org/10.1186/s41239-017-0087-5, under "Introduction"
Fry E, Crewe JC, Wakeford R (2013) Using multiple choice questions to examine the content of the qualifying law degree accurately and reliably: the experience of the Qualified Lawyers Transfer Scheme. Law Teacher 47:234–242
Gadd E, Weedon R (2017) Copyright ownership of E-learning and teaching materials: policy approaches taken by UK universities. Educ Inform Technol 22:3231–3250
Garner D (2000) Socratic misogyny?—analyzing feminist criticisms of socratic teaching in legal education. Brigham Young Univ Law Rev 1597–1649
Guthrie R (2005) Teachers and stress. Aust New Zealand J Legal Educ 5:5–18
Heinrich DRM (2015) Teaching and assessing professional communication skills in law school. North Dakota Law Rev 91:99–130
Hemming A (2010) Online tests and exams: lower standards or improved learning? Law Teacher 44:283–308
Jones D (2019) Legal skills and the SQE: confronting the challenge ahead. Law Teacher 53:35–48
Jones E, Rajvinder S, Lucassen M (2018) The world at their fingertips? the mental well-being of online distance-based law students. Law Teacher 53(1):49–69
Kales AM, Ripley TE (1922) Should the law teacher practice law? Harvard Law Rev 25(3):253–273
Kerr OS (1999) The decline of the socratic method at harvard. Nebraska Law Rev 78:113–134
Liu H-Y (2012) Teaching without authority. Law Teacher 46:146–164
Majid AA (2005) The art of advocacy: an indispensable skill for common law advocates. Eur J Legal Educ 2:39–58
Marton F, Säljö R (1976) On qualitative differences in learning: 1-outcome and process. British J Educ Psychol 46:4–11
Murphy CP, CJ. Ryan Jr, Warnapala Y (2018–19) Note-taking mode and academic performance in two law school courses. J Legal Educ 68:2017–229
Narayandas D, Hebbar V, Li L (June 2020) Lessons from Chinese companies' response to Covid-19. Harvard Bus Rev 5. https://hbr.org/2020/06/lessons-from-chinese-companies-response-to-covid-19
Offer K, Skead N, Seen A (2018) "You must be joking": the role of humour in the law classroom. Law Teacher 52:135–153
Oseid JA (2018) Tale less, smile more. J Legal Educ 68:176–183
Owen R (2013) Best practices: Australian clinical legal education. Law Teacher 47:421–429
Palace VM (2019) What if artificial intelligence wrote this: artificial intelligence and copyright law. Florida Law Rev 71:218–242
Peden JR (1972) Goals for legal education. J Legal Educ 24:379–396
Prosser WL (1948) Lighthouse no good. J Legal Educ 1:257–267
Robert P (2017) Leadership in educational institutions: reflections of a law school dean. Stanford Law Rev 69:1817–1829
Ramsden M, Marsh L (2014) Using clinical education to address an unmet need: a Hong Kong perspective. J Legal Educ 63:447–459
Schneider J (2012) Socrates and the madness of method. Phi Delta Kappa 94:26–29
Sherry CS, Terrill L, Laurens J (2018) (Re)Introducing a closed book exam in law. Legal Educ Rev 28:1–26
Skead N, Elphick L, McGaughey F, Wesson M, Offer K, Montalto M (2020) If your record, they will not come—but does it really matter? Student attendance and lecture recording at an Australian law school. Law Teacher 54:349–367
Smith M (2020) Integrating technology in contemporary legal education. Law Teacher 54:209–221
Tait G (2009) Behaviour disorder and teacher negligence. Int J Law Educ 14:93–102

Tan C-H (2010) The goals and objectives of law schools beyond educating students: research, capacity-building, community service—the national university of singapore school of law experience. Penn State Int Law Rev 29(1):67–79
Tarrant J (2006) Teaching time-savvy law students. James Cook Univ Law Rev 13:64–80
Turner J, Bone A, Ashton J (2018) Reasons why law students should have access to learning law through a skills-based approach. Law Teacher 52:1–16
Whaley DJ (2007) Teaching law: thoughts on retirement. Ohio State Law J 68:1387–1417
Wolff L-C (2020) AI *ante portas*—the end of comparative law?. Chinese J Comp Law 484–504
Wu FH (2016) The end(s) of legal education. J Legal Educ 66:18–23

Books/Book Chapters

Boele-Woelki K (2010) Unifying and harmonizing substantive law and the role of conflict of laws. Martinus Nijhoff Publishers, Leiden/Boston
Boyle F et al (2005) A practical guide to lawyering skills, 3rd edn. Cavendish Publishing Limited, London
Copeland L, Griggs L (1985) Going international: how to make friends and deal effectively with in the global market place. Random House, New York
Deiβner S (2012) Interregionales privatrecht in China (Interregional Law in China). Tübingen, Mohr Siebeck
Finch E, Stefan F (2011) Legal skills, 3rd edn. Oxford University Press, Oxford
Friedland SI, Hess GF (eds) (2004) Teaching the law school curriculum. Carolina Academic Press, Durham: N.C.
Grant E, Simpson S, Kelly T (eds) (2018) Experiential education in the law school curriculum. Carolina Academic Press, Durham: N.C.
Johnstone R (1997) Designing print materials for flexible teaching and learning in law. Cavendish Publishing, Sydney
Kurzweil R (2005) The singularity is near. Viking, New York
Macfarlane J (1993–reprinted 1995) In: Costanzo, Margot, legal writing London: Cavendish Publishing Limited. p. 5
Pope D, Hill D (2011) Mooting and advocacy skills, 2nd edn. Sweet and Maxwell, London
Rice S, Coss G (1996) A Guide to implementing clinical teaching methods in the law school curriculum. Centre for Legal Education, Sydney
Storrs Hall J, Beyond AI (2007) Creating the Conscience of the Machine. Prometheus Books, Amherst, N.Y.
Susskind R (2017) Tomorrow's lawyers, 2nd edn. Oxford University Press, Oxford
Tamanaha B (2012) Failing law schools. University of Chicago Press, Chicago
Tayeb M (2003) Cultural differences across the world. In: Harlow et.al (ed.) International Management. FT Prentice Hall
Villa RA, Jacqueline S, Nevin A (2004) A guide to co-teaching. Corwin Press, Thousand Oaks
Webb J, Maughan C, Maughan M, Keppel-Palmer M, Boon A (2011) Lawyer's skills. Oxford University Press, Oxford
West Rist D, Brand RA (eds) (1988) The export of legal education: its promise and impact in transition countries. Ashgate Publishing Company, Farnham and Burlington
Wolff L-C (2018) The law of cross-border business transactions, 2nd edn. Kluwer Law International, Alphen aan den Rijn
Wolff L-C, Chan J (2016) Flipped classrooms for legal education. Springer, Singapore

Others

Brownlee J (16 Aug 2019) What is deep learning?. https://machinelearningmastery.com/what-is-deep-learning/
Chan YJ Outcome-based education for legal education in Hong Kong—A mixed mode study, Ph.D. thesis project, Faculty of Law—The Chinese university of Hong Kong (forthcoming)
Christine N Hear the oracle speak—Lee Kai-fu forecasts the future of AI, CUHK Newsletter 19 April 2019. p 04. https://www.iso.cuhk.edu.hk/images/publication/newsletter/536/html5/4/#zoom=z
Corporate legal operations consortium (2020). https://cloc.org/what-is-legal-operations/
CUHK engineering media studio (without date). https://studio.erg.cuhk.edu.hk/micro-modules/about-micro-modules
Derell T (3 June 2015) Formative versus Summative assessment: What's the difference?. https://www.aiuniv.edu/blog/2015/june/formative-vs-summative
Driesen G (8 Jan 2016) The difference between blended and hybrid learning. https://www.anewspring.com/blended-and-hybrid-learning/
Galvis SJ, Jr Robert JG, Werner FA (28 Nov 2018) Introduction: effective crisis management in latin America. https://latinlawyer.com/chapter/1177356/introduction-effective-crisis-management-in-latin-america
German Ministry of Education and Research, Path to Professorship (without date). https://www.research-in-germany.org/en/jobs-and-careers/info-for-postdocs-and-junior-researchers/career-paths/path-to-professorship.html
Hardison KPL (without date) What is the difference between art and science?. https://www.enotes.com/homework-help/deference-between-art-science-172919
Ho N (20 Sep 2020) Mutilating corporal punishments and theories of punishment in traditional Chinese legal thought, CUHK law greater China legal history seminar. https://www.law.cuhk.edu.hk/app/greater-china-20190920/
Illinois CITL (without date) Teaching and learning, Problem-Based Learning (PBL). https://citl.illinois.edu/citl-101/teaching-learning/resources/teaching-strategies/problem-based-learning-(pbl)
Koshal (21 July 2011) Difference between science and art. https://www.differencebetween.com/difference-between-science-and-vs-art/
Lam BH, Chan HL (The Hong Kong Institution of Education) (2005–2013). Experiential learning. https://www.eduhk.hk/aclass/Theories/ExperientialLearning.pdf
Legal Tribune Online (without date) Statistik zur 1. Juristischen Staatsprüfung (Statistics relating to the First Legal State Examination). https://www.lto.de/jura/studium-zahlen/erste-juristische-staatspruefung/
Lewis R Clinical legal education revisited, political science 2012. https://orca.cf.ac.uk/27655/1/CLINICED.pdf
Lublin JD Surface and strategic approaches to learning, (online document which is no longer available) quoted by BYU Center for teaching and learning. https://ctl.byu.edu/tip/teaching-deep-learning
Miller S (31 July 2017) Ten things: legal project management for beginners. https://sterlingmiller2014.wordpress.com/2017/07/31/ten-things-legal-project-management-for-beginners/
Sloan K (23 April 2020) Law schools hit by financial fallouts from COVID-19. https://www.law.com/2020/04/23/law-schools-hit-by-financial-fallout-from-covid-19/?slreturn=20200901034142
Teacher Tapp (without date) Can teachers have Tattoos? What does the law say?. https://teachertapp.co.uk/can-teachers-have-tattoos/
The Education University of Hong Kong (without date) What is Outcome-based Learning?. https://www.eduhk.hk/flanobl/view.php?secid=784
The University of Chicago Law School (without date) Paths to law teaching. https://www.law.uchicago.edu/careerservices/pathstolawteachingte
Washington University (without date) Flipping the classroom. https://teaching.washington.edu/topics/engaging-students-in-learning/flipping-the-classroom/

WebFinance Inc., Business Dictionary (2019). https://www.businessdictionary.com/definition/motivation.html
Wolff L-C (12 May 2014) To tweet or not to tweet: keeping students engaged and off social media during class, presentation at the international trademark association (INTA) Annual meeting—adjunct professors special interest group panel, Hong Kong
Yale Law School Career Development Office (2018–19) Entering the law teaching market. https://law.yale.edu/sites/default/files/area/department/cdo/document/cdo_law_teaching_public.pdf
Young SH (April 2016) What's the difference between learning an art and a science?. https://www.scotthyoung.com/blog/2016/04/19/art-v-science/

The manufacturer's authorised representative in the EU is Springer Nature Customer Service Centre GmbH, Europaplatz 3, 69115 Heidelberg, Germany. If you have any concerns regarding our products, please contact ProductSafety@springernature.com

Printed and bound by CPI Group (UK) Ltd, Croydon, CR0 4YY
30/09/2026
02225258-0009